Pastoral Evangelism

Samuel Southard

Pastoral Evangelism

BROADMAN PRESS
Nashville, Tennessee

Library of Congress catalog card number: 62–15327

Printed in the United States of America

Foreword

Pastoral evangelism is the greatest need of this hour. Without pastoral evangelism, there will not be much of any other kind. Many of us who labor in the field of evangelism are happy to help introduce a book with a fresh approach, like the one written here by Samuel Southard.

Many of the books today which deal at all with the psychological approach to conversion leave out entirely the place of the Holy Spirit in the whole matter. To them, it is only a natural thing, but I am happy that Dr. Southard has shown the work of God in conversion. Every pastor who reads this book will find many helpful and profitable suggestions to assist him in his pastoral ministry.

The author has labored tirelessly to present a mature and well-rounded conception of the challenging field of pastoral evangelism. He has called attention to the need of it and has offered timely suggestions as to how to perform it. This book should be of priceless value to those who take advantage of it.

C. E. AUTREY

Director, Department of Evangelism
Baptist Home Mission Board

Preface

In pastors' conferences I have sometimes been asked: "What does pastoral counseling have to do with the salvation of souls? This book is an attempt to show how the spirit and methodology of one type of pastoral psychology may be used in personal interviews with individuals who have not made a commitment of faith in Christ.

As I was beginning to gather material for this manuscript, an experienced pastor and professor told me: "I don't believe that many of our modern pastors have given much thought to the real meaning of conversion." This led me to a historical and theological study of evangelism and conversion. I found that creative evangelists like Whitefield, Edwards, and Finney, plus many pastors of individual congregations, built upon a foundation of pastoral care and church fellowship. This I have called "personal evangelism." But unimaginative imitators in the twentieth century have intensified the promotional aspects of earlier revivalism and ignored the personal spirit of the work and message. The streamlined, compact product is "instant evangelism."

In my attempts to demonstrate that pastoral evangelism was the practice of the patristic church and pioneer American congregations, I am greatly indebted to the following authorities in evangelism, theology, church history, and pastoral care, who have read the manuscript, made corrections, and offered suggestions:

C. E. Autrey and C. Y. Dossey, Division of Evangelism, Southern Baptist Convention; Robert Ferm, Billy Graham Evangelistic Association; William McLoughlin, Brown University; Sabin Landry, W. Morgan Patterson, Dale Moody, W. W. Adams, William Hull, Raymond Brown, Henlee Barnette, Wayne

Oates, Swan Haworth, Southern Baptist Theological Seminary; Franklin Segler, Southwestern Baptist Theological Seminary; Charles L. King, First Presbyterian Church, Houston, Texas; John Claypool, Crescent Hill Baptist Church, Louisville, Kentucky; David Stitt, Austin Presbyterian Seminary, Austin, Texas. Also, I am indebted to Mrs. Mildred Moon, Tifton, Georgia, for her corrections of style and grammar.

SAMUEL SOUTHARD

Contents

Contents

1

Stillborn Men

It is the fourth night of a revival in an open country, one-room Baptist church. Mary Bell and her family are there for the first time during the revival. She is sitting with other teen-age girls.

Immediately after the benediction, the visiting preacher begins to go down the line of girls, asking each one if she is saved. All answer yes except Mary. The preacher asks that the pastor of the church join him in witnessing to this girl. As the three of them talk in the sight of everyone, Mary begins to cry. The preacher asks her to sit down and says:

"Are you a sinner and do you want to be saved?"

"Yes," she answers.

The preacher opens his Bible, reads Scripture passages on God's plan for man's salvation, and pauses. The book is placed so that she can see all the pages.

"Do you understand these, Mary?" She nods.

"Do you believe you are a sinner?" She nods. "Do you believe that God is ready and willing to save you?"

"Yes."

"Will you repent and ask the Lord to save you right now?"

Mary puts her face in her hands and begins to cry again.

The preacher continues: "Now, Mary, say after me, 'O Lord, be merciful to me, a sinner.'" Hesitatingly she does. "Now say, 'I am now trusting Jesus as my Saviour. Amen.'" Mary slowly repeats the words.

The visiting preacher immediately rises from his knees and says, "Now, sister, you are saved because the Bible says that 'whosoever calleth upon the name of the Lord shall be saved.'"

Mary wanders out of the church building.

1

The pastor who stood by tells the rest of the story: "Mary Bell went home that night and neither she nor her parents (both members of the church) have been back since.

"The next day after that service, I called at Mary's home. I related the experience of the previous night to Mrs. Bell because she had already gone out of the church house when Mary's experience took place. She seemed very satisfied and pleased that Mary had made a profession. She apparently had not talked to Mary about it very much, if any.

"Mary then came in and I talked with her, explaining that the next step a Christian ought to take would be to be baptized and join a church. After a prayer I left.

"Although I have visited them many times since then and every time they tell me they are going to get started back, they never have. They seem to be glad to see me and I can detect no resentment or bad feeling toward me or anyone at our church. Since this past Christmas the children occasionally have attended Sunday school at a church which is within walking distance of their home.

"During my last visit to their home, which was about a month ago, Mrs. Bell and her sons were there. During the conversation she told me that Mary had told her that she just did not want to join our church. She said that she held nothing against us, but that she just did not want to join there. Not knowing how to proceed, I just nodded my head and said nothing more about it.

"Of course you can see that I don't agree with, or like, the visiting preacher's witnessing technique. I personally think he has done more harm than good and has retarded my chances of ever working very effectively with this family. It may be though, that I am using him as an excuse for my own failure to make effective contact with Mary or her family."

Did this girl ever have a real chance to become personally acquainted with and accept the forgiveness of Jesus Christ?

Are Good Intentions Enough?

In answering the question about Mary, one might say: "Oh, I'm sure that the visiting evangelist had the best of intentions!"

This comment could be granted as true in many cases. Our difficulty is often not with our intentions but with our ignorance. We want to lead people like Mary to a saving knowledge of Jesus Christ, but how? Without a sympathetic knowledge of personality we may be frustrated on many occasions. Mary will be submissive in the meeting, but when the social pressure is removed, she retreats from a public commitment to Christ. To win Mary, an evangelist needs more than good intentions. He must combine an understanding of individual motivation with the rich resources of Christian faith.

No matter how much the evangelist wishes Mary to be saved, this will not come about because *he* desires it. The great challenge of witnessing is to relate the concrete experience of each man to the saving call of God in Christ. The power that quickens does not reside in the persuasive impulses of the evangelist, but in the Holy Spirit. We are the spiritual attendants (John 3:1–7; 2 Cor. 3:6; 1 Cor. 15:45; Rom. 8:26), the human assistants of God, in this great drama of rebirth. True faith in Christ is a gift. It is donated to the sons of God by adoption, through the Spirit of Christ. It is his Spirit that convicts of sin, leads to repentance, and gives new life. If the evangelist who witnessed to Mary was asked about this, he would surely say "amen." But his practice is not in keeping with his profession. In Mary's case, he ran ahead of the Spirit of God. The Word may have been sown through the sermon, but no one knows if it took root. Instead, men (two of them) trampled it under foot through their mishandling of this sensitive girl. How may we avoid such mistakes in the future?

Stillborn Men

Church surveys testify to the repeated failure of present-day evangelism. In a 1953 study of inactive and nonresident Baptists, C. E. Matthews concluded that "48.4 per cent of the entire membership of Southern Baptist churches is lost to the cause of Christ." [1] As secretary of evangelism for the Home Mission Board, his judgment is impressive: "The most justifiable criticism that can be made of all that Southern Baptists are doing to-

[1] *A Church Revival* (Nashville: Broadman Press, 1955), p. 103.

day is their failure to conserve the results of their evangelistic efforts." [2] The swift slogans and manipulative methods of popular evangelism still may satisfy our pride in sudden statistical success. But there is growing unrest among laymen and unsatisfied longings among pastors for more personal and permanent witnessing.

One reason for uneasiness is the streamlined reception of converts into the church. A ten-second questioning by the pastor has replaced the month-long agonizing of Puritan New England and the congregational examinations of frontier Kentucky. How can church membership mean anything when a walk down the aisle of a church is the only visible requirement of conversion? J. L. Dagg, in an early Southern Baptist manual, stated the problem: "To receive any one on a mere profession of words, without any effort to ascertain whether he understands and feels what he professes, is unfaithfulness to his interests, and the interests of religion." [3]

Another cause for unrest is the manipulative attitudes and techniques of some evangelists. The coercion of children is especially resented. As one pastor put it: "I'm not going to have another evangelist who empties every row in the Junior department. I've had parents and Sunday school teachers on my neck for months about that. I don't blame them. The kids didn't know what hit them."

Statistically, the age of conversion has been steadily dropping in the past two hundred years. Adults were the usual converts in colonial America. In the nineteenth century, adolescence seemed to be the storm and stress period of salvation. By 1959, pastors in western Kentucky could report that most of their converts were between the ages of six and twelve. Today, churches that nominally assent to believer's baptism only are receiving children at an earlier age than that which is acceptable for full membership in churches that sprinkle infants.

A third danger sign is the unfruitful living of those who are

---

[2] *Ibid.*, p. 102.

[3] *A Manual of Theology, Second Part, a Treatise on Church Order* (Charleston: Southern Baptist Publication Society, 1859), p. 269.

supposed to be saved. The historian Henry Commager commented on this deadening negligence:

By every test but that of influence the church had never been stronger than it was at the opening of the twentieth century, and its strength increased steadily. Everyone was a Christian, and almost everyone joined some church, though few for reasons that would have earned them admission to Jonathan Edwards' Northampton congregation. . . . Never before had the church been materially more powerful or spiritually less effective.[4]

A fourth symptom of superficiality is the loss of over half the converts of a revival within a year after they walked down a church aisle and were assured of salvation. The studies in chapter 8 of this book indicate that this is as true of revivals in a local church as it is of community-wide evangelistic meetings. If life ebbs so swiftly from new Christians it is time to examine the conditions under which they experienced the new birth.

The tragic conclusion is that many personalities are mishandled at the time when they should be reborn and neglected in the following days when they should grow in grace. A generation ago, Harold Begbie prepared numerous case histories of "twice-born men." Today, many products of evangelism would have to be labeled "stillborn men."

The Personal Point of View

When 50 per cent of church members appear to be lifeless, something is wrong with the modern theory and practice of conversion. We need to examine the ways in which we witness and the meaning of that witness for those who profess salvation. The way of witnessing can be examined through written interviews in which a pastor or another Christian leader records his actual conversation with a non-Christian. Such personal conversations form the basis for this book. The meaning of conversion for those who are accepted as converts has been the subject of other books which will be mentioned in this and the following chapters. It is not the primary emphasis of the present work.

[4] Henry S. Commager, *National Needs and Remedies*, pp. 203–204.

The purpose of this book is to investigate theologically and psychologically the ways by which a Christian enters the life and thought of a non-Christian as an ambassador for God. The major emphasis will be upon the evangelistic interview, the conversations in which there is an expectation of decision and commitment. The sources for this study will be verbatim evangelistic interviews prepared by theological students and resident pastors.[5] Most of the two hundred interviews read for this research came from senior theological students, between the ages of twenty-three and thirty. Most of them were part-time pastors of country, village, or small congregations in a city. They had served in their present church from one to five years. Other interviews came from resident pastors who were graduates of a theological seminary. Their material forms the basis for chapters 6, 8, and 10. Denominationally, the sources are predominantly Southern Baptist, although several of the interviews quoted in the following chapters came from Methodist or Presbyterian pastors and theological students.

Personal documents have been used by evangelists and psychologists in the best studies of evangelism and conversion. Following the first Great Awakening of the 1740's, Jonathan Edwards wrote his *Narrative* and *Treatise Concerning Religious Affections*. These volumes were based upon his careful examination of candidates for church membership. Observations and examples from the lives of his parishioners fill the books. A hundred years later, Ichabod Spencer prepared a *Pastor's Sketches*. This was a more detailed study of evangelistic work by one New York pastor's conversations with anxious inquirers. Edwards tended to systematize his observations of people under "signs" or evidences of religious affection. Spencer devoted each chapter to his work with an individual.

---

[5] In this book the documents are verbatim accounts of conversations which a pastor has held with a person who is not a Christian. These accounts are written from memory and are not as accurate as electronic transcriptions of conversations which are sometimes made in formal office counseling settings. The documents will therefore reflect more of the pastor's own memory and judgment of what he said than they do of the complete transcription of the conversation.

In 1902, William James used autobiographical sources in *The Varieties of Religious Experience* to demonstrate the conversions of "once-born" and "twice-born" men. Harold Begbie was inspired by James to document the latter type among Salvationists in London. His studies appeared in *Twice-Born Men* and *Souls in Action.*[6]

As a mental hospital chaplain in Illinois, Anton Boisen in *The Exploration of the Inner World* examined conversion and mental illness. This study was very influential in the clinical training movement of theological students, but it has not been followed up by studies of conversion in normal persons.

The Meaning of Pastoral Evangelism

A definition of pastoral evangelism will help to set the sights through which the panorama of interpersonal dialogue will be viewed. "To evangelize," according to the Church of England Commission on Evangelism, "is so to present Christ Jesus in the power of the Holy Spirit, that men shall come to put their trust in God through Him, to accept Him as their Saviour, and serve Him as their King in the fellowship of His Church."[7]

"Pastoral" is the patient attitude of a Christian leader toward persons for whom he feels a specific spiritual responsibility. This attitude reflects both loving care and righteous discipline. "Shepherding" or pastoral attributes of Old Testament prophets included comfort (Isa. 40) and judgment (Isa. 55). Micah stated the Lord's requirement as justice, loving-kindness, and humility (Mic. 6:8).

In the New Testament, those who were pastors entered into the lives of their people with support and discipline. Christian leaders were commanded to "tend the flock" of God (1 Peter 5:2) and "feed [the] lambs" (John 21:15). These supporting attitudes were balanced by the expectation that those who were "over you in the Lord" would admonish and exhort with pa-

---

[6] For a "casework" approach in the 1920's, see C. R. Zahniser, *Casework Evangelism* (Westwood, N. J.: Fleming H. Revell Co., 1928).

[7] *Towards the Conversion of England* (Toronto: J. M. Dent & Sons, 1946), p. 1.

tience (1 Thess. 5:12–14). The word for admonish (*noutheteō*) was also translated in "warn the idle" (v. 14). It conveyed the meaning of warning and instruction.

In his last letter to the Corinthians, Paul cautioned the readers that his attitude might be severe or it might be mild. Much would depend upon the correction of abuses in the church and consent to the authority entrusted to Paul by God (2 Cor. 13). In the pastoral epistles, the work of an evangelist was to preach, urge, convince, rebuke, and exhort with patience (2 Tim. 4:1–5).

To be pastoral, therefore, is to exercise mercy and discipline with patience. The ability to use time redemptively is one distinction of pastoral judgment. Dr. Wayne Oates considers this to be one of the central issues in the letters to Timothy. The "pastoral" evangelist is one who recognizes conversion as a process which must be consummated in God's time (*kairos*) rather than at a convenient hour (*chronos*). Those who patiently wait for God will find that he can transform superficial sympathy into sensitive concern and impulsive condemnation into righteous conviction.

At times, "pastoral" refers to a specific office in the church. But it also is descriptive of an attitude which may be found among all Christian leaders.[8] In this volume, many of the examples come from those who hold the pastoral office, but the major emphasis is upon a pastoral attitude which is shared by laymen and ministers as they participate in the lives of individuals for the sake of Christ.

"Pastoral evangelism" may be defined as a dialogue in which the Christian's actions and attitudes of loving care and righteous discipline, empowered by the Holy Spirit, awaken a non-Christian so that he will receive Christ as divine Saviour and Lord of his life in the Christian fellowship and in the world.

[8] See Seward Hiltner, *Preface to Pastoral Theology* (New York: Abingdon Press, 1958), chap. 1.

2

The Characteristics of Conversion

The objective of Christian witnessing is conversion, the turning to Christ of one who has not acknowledged him as Saviour-Lord. This is more than a psychological experience. To be Christian, the conversion must have the biblical and historical qualities of a new life in Christ. A knowledge of these qualities will assure the evangelist that he is guiding an inquirer toward the living God and may prevent wandering into formless subjectivism. Personal feelings must be related to the facts of Christian faith.

Christian conversion is a pilgrimage initiated by God in which a person commits his life to the transforming power of Christ. It is described in biblical language as being called out of darkness into marvelous light (1 Peter 2:9), a new birth (John 3:3), redemption from all iniquity (Titus 2:14), passage out of death into life (John 5:24), a turn from the power of Satan unto God (Acts 26:18), a new creation (2 Cor. 5:17), a putting off of an old man and a putting on of a new man (Col. 3:9–10), the indwelling of Christ in the heart by faith (Eph. 3:17), a dying and rising again (Rom. 6:2–8). It is a new life in which all the forces of one's being are turned into a new channel.[1]

The Ministry of Jesus

The work of Jesus in the remaking of persons began with a call to all men for repentance. He saw men as self-centered be-

[1] James Hastings (ed.), *Encyclopedia of Religion and Ethics* (New York: Charles Scribner's Sons, 1908), IV, 106.

9

ings, who not only lived for themselves (Mark 7:21 ff.; Matt. 23) but also corrupted the "little ones" for whom they were responsible (Mark 9:42). His most striking judgments were upon those who were reputed to be religious. They glorified self in the name of God (Matt. 6:2 ff.,23; Luke 18:11).

Jesus, therefore, called for a new pattern of life: "Unless you turn and become like children, you will never enter the kingdom of heaven" (Matt. 18:3). The new man was to have the faithful trust of a child in a Heavenly Father who would forgive his sins, deliver him from temptation, and guide him in spirit (Matt. 6:12–13; Luke 11:13). The crowning grace of a converted creature was his love for the unlovely and his sensitive concern for the despised of this earth (Matt. 5:44; 18:21; 25:34 ff.; John 15:12). This included a godly love of self. The believer is not to mortify the flesh for its own sake (Mark 2:15–17).

Repentance was the characteristic response of those who turned to Jesus. At times it was manifest in a new love for people; the sins of a woman were forgiven because she loved much (Luke 7:47). It might take the tangible form of charity for the poor and restoration of money taken by fraud (Luke 19:8–10). On other occasions, suffering people did not cry for their sins, but rather sought out Jesus because of their great need for him (Mark 2:1–12; Luke 18:35–43). This kind of faith was sufficient (Luke 8:48). Disciples were drawn to him because he fulfilled the deepest hopes of their lives (John 1:35–51).

The Apostolic Proclamation

The preaching of the gospel was the chief instrument for conversion in the early days of the church. The sermons recorded in the book of Acts (2:14–39; 3:12–26; 4:8–12; 10:36–43) contained three elements: (1) a claim that the message was the fulfilment of Old Testament prophecy; (2) an exposition of the life, death, and resurrection of Jesus, (3) a summons to repent and accept forgiveness of sins in Jesus the Son of God.[2] The reinforcement of this preaching was the life of believers. Peter be-

[2] Described by A. M. Hunter in *The Message of the New Testament* (Philadelphia: The Westminster Press, 1944), pp. 24–38.

came a man of courage (Acts 2:14 ff.), the disciples healed the sick (Acts 3:1–10), the church shared possessions (Acts 4:32–37). The seal of conversion was the reception of Christ's spirit and baptism (Acts 2:38).

This upsurge of life was molded and stabilized by the church. In this vibrant fellowship men were trained to love and discipline one another (Acts 5:1–11; 6:1–6). Letters of admonition, consolation, and instruction were circulated by the first missionaries. Converts were urged to grow in grace, to love one another (Eph. 3:14–18; 1 Cor. 13; 1 John). Those who drew back from their profession of faith were warned that they crucified the Son of God (Heb. 6:6). Disputes were to be settled in church (1 Cor. 6:1 ff.). The congregation was a school in Christian living for the convert.

Moving from the first to the second century, we find that one function of the patristic church was the examination of candidates for baptism. The Fathers did not take anyone's conversion for granted. The martyr Hippolytus commanded that a person be examined as to why he wished to become a Christian. His own testimony must be supported by witnesses who knew his manner of life. Detailed instructions were given for questions about marriage, occupation, and social life of the candidate for baptism.[3] Sometimes the period of instruction and examination was extended to three years, but a diligent person of good repute might be admitted to the church in less time.[4]

The Reformation of Evangelism

Confession of sins, public commitment to Christ, examination by and communion with the church were characteristics of conversion in the first three centuries. In the following millennium, the emphasis shifted from repentance to penance. Commitment to Christ was defined as submission to a saving institution, the Church. Communion was not a vital fellowship of all believers,

[3] Gregory Dix (ed.), *The Treatise on the Apostolic Tradition of St. Hippolytus of Rome* (New York: The Macmillan Co., 1937), pp. 23–32.

[4] "Constitutions of the Holy Apostles," in A. Roberts and J. Donaldson (eds.), *The Ante-Nicene Fathers* (New York: Christian Literature Co., 1886), VII, 495.

but a sacrament guarded by the clergy.[5] Conversion became a system of spiritual culture in which the sacraments brought grace, the Church forgave sins, and penance earned merit. The ideal "conversion" was the monastic life. This sacerdotal scheme was shaken by Luther's emphasis upon justification by faith. He taught that man was not justified by merit; he does not earn salvation. Instead, man is saved by the free gift of Christ's grace. The result will be a radical change in personality.

Reformation of personality was a Reformation doctrine of conversion. The expectation of a conscious, transforming experience was developed by the Reformers and popularized by the Puritans.[6] The classic allegory of Puritan conversion experience was *The Pilgrim's Progress*. John Bunyan described the struggle of the pilgrim toward salvation, the decisive event of sins forgiven, and the continuing pilgrimage toward the celestial city. In the eighteenth century this evangelical process was the focus of preaching and practice by the Wesleys and Whitefield in England. In America it was viewed in two ways. Among the settled ministers of New England, conversion was a gradual awakening. Jonathan Edwards distrusted sudden experiences. He did not believe that grace completed everything in an instant. There must be permanence, continual conversion, and renovation of nature.[7] On the frontier, conversions of a more sudden and explosive variety were experienced. Evangelists like John McGee "left the pulpit and went through the audience shouting and exhorting with all possible ecstasy and energy and the floor was soon covered with the slain." [8]

The Creation of a Crisis

The pioneer expectation of a climactic decision was given national prominence through the preaching of Charles Finney.

[5] See W. P. Paterson, *Conversion* (London: Hodder & Stoughton, 1939), chap. 4.

[6] K. S. Latourette, "Distinctive Features," *Evangelism* ("Madras Series"), III, 24; Paterson, *ibid.,* p. 106.

[7] Jonathan Edwards, *Religious Affections,* ed. John Smith (New Haven: Yale University Press, 1959), p. 343.

[8] Charles Johnson, *The Frontier Camp Meeting* (Dallas: Southern Methodist University Press, 1955), p. 35.

As the climax of his famous sermon "Sinners Bound to Change Their Own Hearts," he cried: "Another moment's delay and it may be too late forever." [9]

Finney called for those who knew they were sinners to stand in the audience and come to a separate room for inquiry. This was a bold development of the frontier Methodist and Baptist call for sinners to kneel by the pulpit or sit on the "mourner's bench." [10] The practice was vigorously denounced by conservative pastors. They felt that the call for immediate decision created artificial pressure. Appeals of fear created unstable emotions; conversions did not last. Furthermore, "it is a vastly more easy thing to carry forward the work of religion in this way than it is to be steadily and diligently true to the details of ministerial duty, as prescribed by the Apostle Paul." [11]

The call for an open decision before the church at the conclusion of a sermon was a new evangelistic method. The more traditional method of Edwards and Spurgeon was to preach for a decision and invite those who were convicted to retire after the service to another room in the church or to come on Monday to the pastor's home. After proper inquiry by the pastor, these persons would be presented to the church for membership.[12]

This method was modified in nineteenth-century evangelism. Finney and Moody gave a public invitation at the conclusion of their sermons for inquirers to come to the front during the singing of a hymn. The inquirers went immediately into an "inquiry room." Moody trained a corps of personal workers in each city to counsel those who came to the inquiry room.[13] Under this rapid system, persons soon began to equate the open decision

[9] William McLoughlin, *Modern Revivalism* (New York: The Ronald Press, 1958), pp. 66–72.

[10] Howard Olive, "The Development of the Evangelistic Invitation" (Master's thesis, Southern Baptist Theological Seminary, Louisville, Ky., 1958), p. 29. See also Henry R. McLindon, "The Mourner's Bench" (Th.D. dissertation, Southern Baptist Theological Seminary, Louisville, Ky., 1902).

[11] J. W. Nevin, *The Anxious Bench* (Chambersburg, Pa.: Publication Office, German Reformed Church, 1844), p. 58.

[12] Ola E. Winslow, *Jonathan Edwards, 1703–58* (New York: The Macmillan Co., 1940), p. 163.

[13] B. A. Weisberger, *They Gathered at the River* (Boston: Little, Brown & Co., 1958), pp. 111, 207.

with full *conversion*. In the more traditional method it was a sign of *conviction*, a first step in conversion.

These "new measures" proved to be so popular that evangelism was soon identified with revivalistic methodology: the public invitation or "altar call," the "inquiry room" or "anxious seat," and the assurance of salvation to the inquirer at the time of his public decision. In the twentieth century, personal counsel of the inquirer was guided by "the plan of salvation" which will be discussed in the next chapter.

The psychological impact of these measures was to precipitate an immediate crisis in the lives of unsaved persons. This was so intimately associated with revivalism in 1899 that Edwin Starbuck classified climactic conversions as the "revival experience type." [14] Robert Ferm stated that such "conversions in the New Testament took place at a specific, decisive moment." [15] Those who believe in conversion as a process have failed "to reckon with the activity of the Holy Spirit." [16] Ferm persisted in this exclusive definition despite the evidence of his own questionnaire that 45 per cent of the respondents whose conversions he believed to be genuine, reported "a gradual or an extremely mild conversion." This was explained away by Ferm's assumption that these respondents had been young at the time of their decision to become a Christian and therefore could not remember their crisis experience.[17]

Several factors seem to increase the number of persons who have an intense emotional crisis which is followed by a definite change of attitude. In Starbuck's study, age was stressed. Adolescence was the time of storm and stress; conversion shortened this period by bringing one to a definite crisis.[18] E. T. Clark added another influence, theology. Out of 2,174 cases surveyed, only 6.7 per cent reported a definitive crisis experience. But of

[14] *The Psychology of Religion* (New York: Charles Scribner's Sons, 1901), pp. 67 ff.
[15] *The Psychology of Christian Conversion* (Westwood, N. J.: Fleming H. Revell Co., 1959), p. 187.
[16] *Ibid.*, p. 180.
[17] *Ibid.*, p. 144.
[18] Starbuck, *ibid.*, p. 224.

those raised under a "stern theology," 34.6 per cent experienced a climactic conversion.[19]

A third factor is the personality of the convert. William James discussed this under the categories of "healthy-mindedness" and "the sick soul." His choice of terms refers to a person's natural disposition or attitude toward himself; it is a psychological description of a subjective state, not a theological evaluation. The healthy-minded man is happy, though born only once. He has a sense of union with God that comes by optimistic self-affirmation of divine qualities. There is no writhing under conviction of sin. Conviction belongs to "sick" souls, persons who are persuaded that life is essentially evil. Their lives are stamped with failure.

In a paragraph that mirrors his own personality, James wrote: "The normal process of life contains moments as bad as any of those which insane melancholy is filled with, moments in which radical evil gets its innings and takes its solid turn."[20] To James, the completest religions are those in which the pessimistic elements are best developed. Christianity is such a religion of deliverance.

The "second birth" is an experience of the sick soul. In this conversion the divided self is unified in consequence of its firmer hold upon religious realities. The experience may be gradual or sudden.[21] Religious aims become the habitual center of personal energy.[22]

Anton Boisen approached conversion from the point of view of mentally ill persons. He distinguished three reactions to the threat of personal failure: drifting, concealment, and confronta-

[19] E. T. Clark, *The Psychology of Religious Awakening* (New York: The Macmillan Co., 1929), p. 86; John Holliday found that 93 per cent of professors and students in Moody Bible Institute and other schools of very conservative theology could identify place and date of conversion, *Life from Above* (Toronto: Evangelical Publishers, 1957), p. 135. W. H. Clark has noted that crisis conversion is more than six times as prevalent among religious workers than among converts who are not. *The Psychology of Religion* (New York: The Macmillan Co., 1958), p. 214.

[20] William James, *The Varieties of Religious Experience* (New York: Modern Library, 1902), p. 163.

[21] *Ibid.*, pp. 183, 186.

[22] *Ibid.*, p. 193.

tion. Persons in the last of these patterns proved most open to experiences that were similar to the conversion of the prophets and other "successful explorers" like John Bunyan or George Fox. Patients who tended to confront their faults honestly often entered a panic reaction which produced a change either for the better or for the worse. They did not drift.[23] Those who follow Boisen's categories today may find that a definite conversion experience with strong emotion is most characteristic of those who openly confront their failures. Several studies indicate that emotional crisis is most characteristic of adult conversion.[24] All of Boisen's patients were adults.

The Variety of Conversion Experiences

When surveys are made in individual churches, more than one type of conversion experience is presented. The variety of ages, theological background, and personality patterns produce two general categories: gradual and sudden regeneration. In a questionnaire completed by the men's Bible classes of four rural Kentucky Baptist churches, Luther Buller found that eighteen out of twenty-six respondents thought of their conversion as gradual and growing. Most of them for several years had thought about salvation before they made a public profession of faith.[25] After their public profession, they described conversion as a continuing activity. One wrote: "Whether the experience took place in a Sunday school classroom, church service, or at my mother's knee would be impossible to say." Another said: "I let my business problems get the best of me. I would often feel empty inside with no hope in sight. Then I would feel a new awareness of God's holding out his hand if I would only take it. Thus I believe conversion experiences are taking place at all times."

Theologians who have been active in evangelism have recognized the individual differences in the process of regeneration. E. Y. Mullins wrote:

[23] Anton Boisen, *The Exploration of the Inner World* (New York: Harper & Brothers, 1936), pp. 40–57.

[24] E. T. Clark, *op. cit.,* pp. 47 ff.; Ferm, *op. cit.,* p. 86.

[25] Sixty years previously, Starbuck, *op. cit.,* p. 67, reported that the average period of conviction before climax of conversion was 47 weeks.

While repentance and faith are central and essential in every conversion, there are many varieties in the experience of those who find Christ. The point of emphasis varies with the individual. With some love seems to be the dominating motive. With others it is obedience, with others hope; and in some cases merely the desire to do right is the chief motive.[26]

Individual differences in religious awakenings are recognized by revivalists such as Robert Ferm. Although Mr. Ferm insists upon a definite turning point from unbelief to belief, he warns against the dogmatic assertion that one must experience one particular brand of conversion in order to be accepted:

Such standardization causes some persons to seek desperately to duplicate the prescribed upheaval, and it begets superficiality and hypocrisy, because the subjects may claim for themselves a pseudo-conversion in order to be accepted by the group. It also erects barriers to certain personality types who are psychologically incapable of experiencing conversion in accordance with the defined standard.[27]

In the New Testament we find a variegated treasure of experiences with Christ. John, Andrew, and Peter came to Jesus out of wonder, admiration, and a sense of life fulfilment (John 1:35–51); the Philippian jailer found salvation in the midst of a cataclysmic experience (Acts 16:19–34); the Samaritan woman went away from Jesus asking a question: "Can this be the Christ?" (John 4:29). There is no *one* method of biblical evangelism. Nineteenth-century revivalistic techniques are not the mold into which all the richness of biblical narratives must be compressed.

The Decisiveness of Christian Commitment

The identification of evangelism with a cataclysmic experience and a stereotyped methodology has caused some pastors to reject all "revivalism." In so doing, they have often neglected the bibli-

---

[26] E. Y. Mullins, *Talks on Soul Winning* (Nashville: Convention Press, 1920), p. 18.

[27] Ferm, *op. cit.*, p. 217.

cal emphasis upon a conscious decision for Christ. Commitment and dedication are essential elements of the Christian life. They are based upon an Old Testament heritage (e.g., Josh. 24:15) and a New Testament fulfilment (John 7:37–38, for the words of Jesus; and Acts 2 for an apostolic sermon). For some persons the decision for Christ comes abruptly and explosively; for others it is the quiet culmination of convictions that matured over a period of months or years. In either case, there is a time when one must identify himself. "Who am I before God and his people?" is the question that requires private and public affirmation.

The decisiveness of conversion may be compared to the vows of marriage.[28] Falling in love may be sudden or gradual. There may be a quiet tenderness or a rush of emotion in the first avowals of love. Whatever the feelings may be, there comes a time for the question: "Will you marry me?" There is a day of decision, a moment before the altar when a man and a woman take public and private responsibility for each other as one flesh. In some instances it may be years before the full impact of love dawns upon one or both partners. But the awareness may come because they were dedicated to that expectation in the marriage ceremony and personal relationship.

In the same way, men are led through unique patterns of emotion to the foot of the cross. Yet upon each one is placed the necessity for a mature, manly choice: "Whom do *you* say that I am?" The answer must always be the same: "The Christ of God" (Luke 9:20), but the way in which a man finds that answer will be his own. In the process of new birth, the Spirit of God is as free as the wind (John 3:8).

The Pilgrim's Progress

Conversion may be described as the beginning of a pilgrimage toward God. It involves a view concerning the past, the present, and the future. Salvation as a past event is described

---

[28] Marriage has been presented as a type of the divine-human encounter in Hosea and Ephesians; the Song of Solomon has traditionally been interpreted as having this meaning.

theologically as redemption, justification, or reconciliation.[29] In the thought of the apostle Paul, Christ has already reconciled us to God (2 Cor. 5:16–21); enslavement to sin has already been broken (Rom. 3:19–26); the revelation of God's righteousness in Christ has provided justification, the grounds for right relations with God (Rom. 5:1–21). When a Christian looks to the past, therefore, he considers the gracious acts of God in history and the stirrings of the Holy Spirit in his own life toward redemption.

Conversion as a present experience is the intimate fellowship of a believer with Christ and his people. It is not a mourning memory for a "mountaintop" experience in the past, but a divine power for new life today (1 Thess. 1:5; Rom. 15:13). Now, in this present time, the Christian is renewed (2 Cor. 4:10–18) and quickened (Eph. 2:1). He looks for an abundant life in his present relationships.

"Salvation is an act, a process, and a consummation." [30] As a progressive experience, the conversion implies present commitment and future hope: "Work out your own salvation with fear and trembling; for God is at work in you" (Phil. 2:12–13). The Christian presses on toward the completion of his redemption (1 Cor. 15:42–58; Phil. 3:12–16). He does not yet know what God will make of him; it is enough to know that he is being remade in the image of God's Son.

These three aspects of conversion are inseparable. This full experience of salvation is reduced when one thinks of conversion as an experience he "once had." How can one assure others that he is a Christian when he crucifies Christ by his present neglect? Past promises are not enough. Nor can future expectations be all that the new life holds for a convert. "Pie in the sky" is no substitute for a transformation of present attitudes. The eternal "now" of God requires that men look to the future for the consummation of activities which they undertake in his name to-

---

[29] A. M. Hunter, *Interpreting Paul's Gospel* (Philadelphia: The Westminster Press, 1955), p. 32.

[30] W. T. Conner, *The Gospel of Redemption* (Nashville: Broadman Press, 1945), p. 139.

day. "Salvation involved a great deliverance in the past, a rich experience in the present, and a confident hope for the future —all made possible through the death and resurrection of Christ." [31]

The Fruit of the Spirit

The fruition of spiritual birth is "to grow up in every way into him who is the head, into Christ" (Eph. 4:15). A regenerate life is the fruit of the Spirit (Gal. 5:16–24). The quality of new attitudes is the visible sign of conversion. Like a skilful physician, pastors must know the signs of spiritual growth and decay among those who inquire after salvation. E. Y. Mullins called this "spiritual diagnosis." [32] What are the characteristics of a fruitful conversion? [33]

A Christ-like conversion experience is well defined.—The person is able to tell how his life is different. One of the men who was interviewed by Mr. Buller said, "I realized that I was on the wrong path and began immediately to improve my conduct." Another one said, "My conversion was like a burden lifted off my shoulders and everything took on a new meaning." If a man describes his conversion as a gradual process, he should be able to state how this way of looking at things is different from that of persons who are not allied with Christ.

A maturing conversion is full of life.—It is a growing experience. Paul wrote to the Philippians that those who are mature will "press on toward the goal for the prize of the upward call of God in Christ Jesus" (Phil. 3:14). The new Christian does not take his conversion for granted. He is continually discovering new ways in which his life may be changed for the glory of God.

A fruitful conversion produces a consistent morality.—The writer to the Hebrews warned that those who "go on to ma-

[31] F. W. Dillistone, *The Significance of the Cross* (Philadelphia: The Westminster Press, 1944), p. 48.

[32] *The Christian Religion in Its Doctrinal Expression* (Philadelphia: Judson Press, 1917), p. 60. An eighteenth-century example of such diagnosis is Jonathan Edwards' *Religious Affections, op. cit.*

[33] I am indebted to Dr. Gordon Allport of Harvard's Department of Psychology, who has described in *The Individual and His Religion* (New York: The Macmillan Co., 1950) six characteristics of a mature religious sentiment.

turity" will not crucify the Son of God again by holding him up to contempt (Heb. 6:1–8). A dynamic Christian experience will enable a man to examine one area of life after another in the Spirit of Christ. Ancient prejudices, lifelong pride, and secret habits will be transformed into loving attitudes toward others.

The mature conversion is comprehensive.—The saved person does not confine his faith to one narrow channel of life. He must examine his business practices, his family responsibilities, his social and racial attitudes in the light of Christ's pure love. Jesus denounced those who neglected justice and mercy and faith (Matt. 23:23–24).

Each part of a man's religious experience is closely connected to every other part.—The person who has experienced the new birth can see how the judgment and love of God are connected. He does not exalt one part of God's being over another. He is able to explain Old Testament views of God in the light of Christ's full revelation in the New Testament. He does not follow the example of Thomas Jefferson, who printed the Four Gospels from which all of the miraculous stories had been excluded. Instead, his faith is integrated; it all hangs together.

The mature convert is a humble learner.—He does not boast about his new knowledge in Christ nor act as though he knows all things. He does not magnify his certainties to condemn all differences. The apostle Paul warned those who were arrogant that "the kingdom of God does not consist in talk but in power" (1 Cor. 4:20). In a growing Christian experience, the convert is always ready to learn some new truth. He examines his previous convictions and discards those which are not in keeping with a deeper Christian faith.

Such conversions are the source of the theological and psychological characteristics of a shift in loyalty toward Jesus Christ. In the fruits of these attitudes men can taste the true flavor of Christian living.

By contrast, there are other "conversions" that move tragically away from the Spirit of Christ.[34]

---

[34] These are adapted from the article of Dr. Leon Salzman, "The Psychology of Religious and Ideological Conversion," *Psychiatry*, XVI: 177–87.

1. Conversions that move away from Christ may begin with an exaggerated zeal. The "convert" tries to do everything. Nothing is considered to be impossible, and all must be done today. This is often followed by an abrupt coolness and lack of interest in the new faith. Like the seed that fell on stony ground, these converts have no roots. The zealot may condemn Christians who do not immediately share all of his enthusiasm. But tomorrow his story is different. Sudden obstacles have arisen to cool his ardor. He has become a perennial backslider, yet it is difficult to convict him of sin. He still remains as a nominal member of the church.

2. The stillborn convert is preoccupied with the form of religion. He shows little interest in the great principles of the faith. He quickly develops a religion "of good works." Although he is a new member of the church, he immediately begins to test everyone for his orthodoxy. He becomes greatly disturbed by any change in the order of worship, reading from a new translation of the Bible, or the buying of different hymnals. Yet he can give no reason for his opposition that is consistent with Christian doctrine.

3. The regressive convert hates everyone who was connected with his former way of life. Instead of confessing his sins as a responsible adult, he may turn on his parents and viciously denounce them. All blame for his former actions is placed upon others. His "holier than thou" attitude turns his acquaintances against him. They are not won to Christ by the transforming love of his new life. Instead, they are repulsed by the hateful and sarcastic words with which he now denounces them. This man cannot forgive himself. He is furious with himself for having lived as he did, yet he will not let God forgive him and show him a better way of life. His "conversion" is just one more weapon with which he justifies his contempt for people.

4. An abortive conversion magnifies spiritual pride. The convert who is filled with self-love will be intolerant of anyone who disagrees with his position. If the pastor tries to explain that there are varying interpretations of particular Scripture passages, the man will denounce the pastor. The "convert" may take a

Sunday school teacher to task for some imagined difference of opinion. He may even go uninvited to the homes of deacons and upbraid them for not living as he does.

5. The ungodly convert rushes toward martyrdom. His attitudes deliberately provoke attacks from others. It is easy to see how the characteristics just described would cause many persons to become infuriated with such a "convert." When people have had enough of this kind of conduct, they will turn on such a man. He will glory in this. To him, it is absolute proof that he alone is righteous. Everyone else is a sinner. They are persecuting him because of his faith.

6. The misguided convert may abandon all family responsibilities. He will behave like Jerome and other monks of the Middle Ages. He may completely give up time he may have spent with his children and excuse himself by saying that he is too busy at the church. If it is a woman, she may wander about the community, gossiping with anyone who will listen, while her husband and children shift for themselves. Both the theology and practice of the New Testament speak against these people. The author of the Pastorals instructs Timothy to see that widows "first learn their religious duty to their own family" (1 Tim. 5:4). Those who forbid marriage are "giving heed to deceitful spirits and doctrines of demons" (1 Tim. 4:1). The roots of the Roman Catholic perversion of marriage have been traced by D. S. Bailey in *Sexual Relations in Christian Thought*.

These characteristics of unfruitful conversion are the opposite of Christ's spirit. They must be identified and challenged, just as the signs of fruitful conversion are to be seen and encouraged. "Not every one who says to me, 'Lord, Lord,' shall enter the kingdom of heaven, but he who does the will of my Father who is in heaven" (Matt. 7:21).

3

Instant Evangelism

"Instant evangelism" is an urgent and individualistic appeal for salvation.[1] In this form of witnessing, the hearer is asked to make an immediate decision for Christ. This decision is to be stated verbally as a surrender of the will to God. Once this is said, the witness assures the person that he is saved. The conversation is concentrated upon theological questions and biblical quotations which are arranged into a "plan of salvation." Few if any questions are raised about the hearer's past, his present relationship to family and community, or his future hopes.

The Frontier Pattern

This type of evangelism grew out of the frontier religion of the early nineteenth century. As has been noted in the previous chapter, camp-meeting preachers sought to create an immediate crisis in the lives of the unsaved. The resolution of this crisis came through private and public profession of faith in Christ. The anxious bench and the inquiry room were aids provided by the church to the inquirer.

What happened after the inquirer had "professed religion"? On the frontier, this was only one step in the process of salvation. In fact, even this initial expression of feeling was closely watched. Jesse Lee wrote in 1806 that laymen were stationed throughout the audience to watch those who seemed to have entered a spiritual crisis. The laymen were well acquainted with

[1] "Instant" is used as a descriptive rather than as a derogatory adjective. It is chosen because the major emphasis of such interviews is upon an *immediate* decision. "Instantaneous" is a word often used by revivalists to describe the activity of the Holy Spirit in conversion. For example, see Ferm, *op. cit.*, p. 180.

24

the people and could "tell pretty well whether they were deceived or not." [2] Only those whose profession seemed to be genuine were encouraged to seek church membership. Lists of converts were prepared at Methodist camp meetings by these laymen and preachers. The names of converts were then given to class leaders who would instruct them for six months before they were received into the church. During many meetings, the presiding elder would speak to the inquirers who had gathered in the "pen," an enclosure next to the preacher's "stand." He outlined their probationary period and discussed the Methodist discipline by which they must live and be judged.[3]

Frontier Presbyterians were as cautious, if not more so, than the Methodists. Neither Presbyterians, Methodists, nor Baptists equated the emotional upheavals of a revival with salvation, although Presbyterians like James McGready encouraged emotional expression. McGready was pleased to see "the floor covered with the slain" during his exhortation. But he also noted after the meeting that there were only "about" ten converts.[4] These converts were received into the church at the communion service which was the stated occasion for a frontier Presbyterian gathering. The revival "manifestations" were encouraged on the weekend before the Sunday communion. Those who professed faith during the revival were examined by the pastors as a prerequisite to church membership.

Three steps were required by Presbyterians in frontier Indiana. First, the candidate was expected to be under conviction of sin; second, there was to be some assurance of salvation; third, there was formal examination of the candidate by the session and admission to the Lord's Supper. It was very rare for a person to achieve all three steps during one revival-communion meeting. Ministers and elders were cautioned against the hasty receipt of new members. As a safeguard, the names of candidates were published for some weeks and elders were to converse frequently with them. Pastors discreetly sought to discourage those who believed "that all they have to do to be saved is to join the meeting, partake of the ordinance of God's house, and do a little *better*." [5] Professor L. C. Rudolph concluded that among frontier Indiana Presbyterians, "the proportion seems always to be many anxious, some hopeful, and few or none received." [6]

Baptists received members more quickly than Methodists or Presbyterians. At the conclusion of a sermon, a Baptist minister would "open the door to hear experiences." On such an occasion in 1812, Jacob Bower rose to tell of his month-long struggle toward salvation. When he had finished, the moderator of the church said, "Can any person forbid water?" and the members rushed to Jacob with joy. [7]

The relating of a "Christian experience" was the public highlight of a conversion in a Baptist congregation. A Georgia pastor, the Rev. S. G. Hillyer, recalled that in the 1800's it was the custom for Baptists everywhere to require this recital of conversion before the church. This "affords a credible and reasonable evidence of a genuine conversion." [8] In support of this practice, Mr. Hillyer told how his mother was skeptical when a middle-aged Negro came forward to make his profession. But when the church had heard him, they received him gladly. She was so impressed by this that she soon made her own declaration of faith. [9] The public testimony was thus a means of inspiration to the church as well as a time of examination for the candidate.

After the candidate had given his public testimony, members of the congregation asked him questions. The reasons for this were given in a *Manual of Theology*,

The churches are not infallible judges, being unable to search the heart; but they owe it to the cause of Christ, and to the candidate him-

---

[5] Letter of Absalom Peters (1838) quoted in L. C. Rudolph, "Hoosier Zion," (Ph.D. dissertation, Yale University, New Haven, Conn., 1958), p. 177.

[6] *Ibid.*, p. 178.

[7] "Autobiography of Jacob Bower," in W. W. Sweet, *The Baptists* (New York: Henry Holt & Co., 1931), p. 199.

[8] S. G. Hillyer, *Reminiscences of Georgia Baptists* (Atlanta: Foote & Davies, 1902), p. 182.

[9] *Ibid.*, p. 185.

self, to exercise the best judgment of which they are capable. To receive anyone on a mere profession of words, without any effort to ascertain whether he understands and feels what he professes, is unfaithfulness to his interests, and the interests of religion. In primitive times, when persecution deterred from profession, and when the Spirit operated in a more visible manner, the danger of mistake was less; but even then, all who professed were not received. John the Baptist rejected some from baptism, who did not bring forth fruits meet for repentance. They who are unfit for baptism, are unfit for church-membership.[10]

This polity was in force on the frontier. On the day Jacob Bower was received for baptism, sixteen others made profession. Two were rejected after examination by pastor and congregation.[11]

In preparation for the public testimony, candidates were advised to counsel privately with the pastor. In the *Baptist Confession of Faith and a Summary of Church Discipline* (Charleston, S. C., 1831), the "admission of members" began with pastoral counsel. The minister would encourage or discourage the candidate. Those who were encouraged would then be examined before the church on the basis of their godly experience, soundness of faith, and regular life.[12]

On the frontier, the pastor often talked with the candidates in or near the log cabin where the revival service was held. In 1772, John Taylor sat close to the minister who was examining eight candidates for baptism. Taylor was in such inner turmoil that he concluded that only one of the eight was a Christian. But on the next day "a tide of heavenly joy" flowed into him and he saw that his fellow candidates were saved as he was. Two weeks later he was baptized.[13]

Despite the safeguards of private counsel by the pastor and public examination by the church, many revival converts were unstable in their profession.[14] Baptists sought to remedy this by

[10] Dagg, *op. cit.*, p. 269.
[11] Sweet, *op. cit.*, p. 199.
[12] *Baptist Confession of Faith and a Summary of Church Discipline* (Charleston: W. Riley, 1831), pp. 215–16.
[13] Sweet, *op. cit.*, pp. 114–15.
[14] W. B. Posey, *The Baptist Church in the Lower Mississippi Valley, 1776–1845* (Lexington: University of Kentucky Press, 1957), p. 56.

strict discipline. In some churches this was reformative; the members were carefully sought out, counseled, and received into the fellowship.[15] Abbreviated records of other churches tend to indicate swift and arbitrary judgment upon the offender.[16] After examining the minutes of many frontier Baptist churches, Professor Posey concluded: "Scarcely a minute book examined does not contain a report of some misconduct considered at each meeting." [17]

These records from Baptist, Presbyterian, and Methodist sources indicate that frontier evangelism contained the following elements: (1) personal conviction of sin; (2) personal assurance of salvation; (3) preaching for conviction of sin and salvation, followed by public invitations from the pulpit to inquire further into religion or to recount a saving experience at the conclusion of the service; (4) private examination of the candidate by the pastor; (5) public examination of the candidate by the church or session; (6) a probationary and instruction period before church membership (Methodist and Presbyterian) or discipline of members after they were received (Baptist).

In the twentieth century instant evangelism has retained an emphasis upon personal conviction of sin and assurance of salvation. The public invitation has been intensified. Instead of an invitation to inquiry or testimony, many modern evangelists equate a public decision with full salvation. This is the heritage of Finney. Private and public examinations are usually abbreviated into a ten-second conversation with the candidate near the pulpit. The congregation remains seated with the expectation that the minister will immediately recommend the candidate for baptism and church membership. The probationary and instruction period is retained by some churches. Disciplinary action regarding misconduct is almost forgotten. It appears, therefore, that modern instant evangelism has only half the heritage of pioneer religion.

---

[15] E.g., "Severns Valley Church Record," Sweet, *op. cit.,* pp. 256, 260, 261.
[16] E.g., "Records of the Forks of Elkhorn Baptist Church," Sweet, *op. cit.,* pp. 273, 282–83.
[17] Posey, *op. cit.,* p. 39.

The Plan of Salvation

Without the safeguards of previous generations, how can modern evangelists assure a person of instant salvation? Two guarantees have been developed in the twentieth century: (1) the plan of salvation to guide the evangelist and (2) verbal assent to this plan by the inquirer.

The "plan of salvation" is a phrase with many meanings. Among the Disciples of the early nineteenth century, the "plan" meant that baptism preceded remission of sins and the gift of the Holy Spirit.[18] In strict Calvinism it was synonymous with the "order of decrees," the process by which God determined the redemption of the world.[19] James Walker's *Philosophy of the Plan of Salvation* (1887) was a general title for theology focused upon personal salvation. Sermons which emphasized God's desire for man's redemption might bear the title *Twelve Sermons on the Plan of Salvation* (C. H. Spurgeon, 1892). The "plan of salvation" was a phrase that might be heard in many churches of the late nineteenth and early twentieth centuries.[20]

In the evangelism of previous generations this phrase did not indicate a step-by-step, rigid system of conversion. In his exhaustive investigation of the signs of salvation, Jonathan Edwards (1746) stated that there was no definite order in the process by which a man develops the "new sense" of God.[21] A hundred years later Charles Finney presented a variety of methods by which God's grace might be mediated to sinners. He classified sinners as awakened, careless, and convicted. He felt that no two could be dealt with in the same way. "Great evils have arisen, and many false hopes have been created by not

---

[18] Jesse R. Kellems, *Alexander Campbell and the Disciples* (New York: Richard R. Smith, Inc., 1930), p. 193. This "plan" was vigorously rejected by the Baptists, who follow the plan of Crouch described below.

[19] Benjamin Warfield, *The Plan of Salvation* (Grand Rapids: Wm. B. Eerdmans Publishing Co., 1942), pp. 13, 101; "By the decrees of God we mean that eternal plan by which God has rendered certain all the events of the universe, past, present, and future." A. H. Strong, *Systematic Theology* (New York: Press of E. R. Andrews, 1886), p. 171.

[20] Personal correspondence with C. E. Autrey, Division of Evangelism, Southern Baptist Convention.

[21] Edwards, *op. cit.*, pp. 20–21, 30.

discriminating between an awakened and a convicted sinner." [22]
Indiscriminate exhortations to repent have greatly injured revivals.

It appears that other evangelists of the nineteenth century
shared this diagnostic approach to conversion. Neither Moody
nor Spurgeon advised a rigid "plan" in their talks to Christians
who would witness to others.[23] Moody's flexible spirit is indicated by his admonition that God never repeats himself; he does
not approach any two people the same way. "What I want first
to call your attention to, if you are going to be successful in
winning souls to Christ, is the need for discrimination in finding
out people's differences." [24]

When specific steps were suggested, as in Torrey's *How to Work
for Christ,* they were first classified as "How to deal with those
who realize their need of a Saviour and really desire to be
saved." [25] Other suggestions were offered in the following chapters for other types of witnessing.

Theologians who discussed the "order of salvation" were careful to point out that there was no rigid system of salvation: "The
doctrine of conviction should not be made into a stereotyped
rule. We are not to suppose that all men are required to pass
through a conscious and clearly defined conviction of sin, of
righteousness, and of judgment in explicit terms." [26] Mullins affirmed the instantaneous work of God in salvation,[27] but rejected
a swift, stereotyped, superficial assurance of salvation to the
inquirer.

As the twentieth century progressed, these flexible approaches
to "soul-winning" diminished among the inheritors of the frontier tradition. While one group of Christians moved away from

[22] Charles G. Finney, *Lectures on Revivals of Religion* (Cambridge: Harvard University Press, 1960), pp. 164, 149–56.
[23] Charles Spurgeon, *The Soul-Winner* (Westwood, N. J.: Fleming H. Revell
Co., 1895); Dwight L. Moody, *Glad Tidings* (New York: E. B. Treat & Co.,
1876), pp. 461 ff.
[24] Dwight L. Moody, *Great Joy* (New York: E. B. Treat & Co., 1877),
p. 277.
[25] R. A. Torrey, *How to Work for Christ* (Westwood, N. J.: Fleming H.
Revell Co., 1901), pp. 39–49.
[26] Mullins, *The Christian Religion in Its Doctrinal Expression,* pp. 367–68.
[27] *Ibid.,* p. 382.

any crisis experience, another group developed a stylized system of salvation as a part of the crisis. In the first part of this century the two groups were moving apart. The "plan of salvation" was at times a necessary bulwark against the humanistic tendencies of works like *The Finality of the Christian Religion* (1909). The author, George Foster, was disfellowshiped from the Chicago Baptist Ministers' Conference for his repudiation of the "Bible plan of salvation." [28]

By the 1920's the "plan of salvation" was systematized and applied to personal witnessing. One popular example of this new trend was Austin Crouch's *Plan of Salvation* (1924). Conversion was condensed into a five-step outline:

1. Show the one with whom you are dealing that he is a sinner and therefore lost.
2. Show the one with whom you are dealing that he cannot save himself.
3. Show the one with whom you are dealing that Christ can save him.
4. Show the one with whom you are dealing that Christ will save him on two conditions (repentance and faith).
5. Show the one with whom you are dealing the duty of a believer in Christ (it is the duty of Christians to serve Christ; the faithful servant will be rewarded when the Master comes; the disobedient servant will be chastised in this life).[29]

In each chapter, Scripture passages and personal conversations were offered as guides for the witness.

All of Crouch's points were in previous evangelical treatises. But there were two differences. First, the new "plan" was more condensed and rigid than earlier works. Second, it made no reference to the various conditions of men and assumed that one approach was satisfactory for all. This was contradictory to the methodology and spirit of Edwards, Finney, Moody, Spurgeon, and Mullins. Yet the twentieth-century plan has been widely

[28] Stewart G. Cole, *The History of Fundamentalism* (New York: Richard R. Smith, Inc., 1931), p. 90.
[29] Austin Crouch, *The Plan of Salvation* (Nashville: Sunday School Board of the Southern Baptist Convention, 1924), chapter headings and subtitles.

adopted by many evangelical groups. Crouch's outline is similar
to that used by Professor E. M. Harrison of Wheaton in *How to
Win Souls* (1952). Mimeographed materials for "personal
workers" in Billy Graham campaigns have advised, "Present the
plan of salvation."

In practice, the plan is often introduced by a question like:
"Do you believe that this book (the Bible) is God's Word?" If
the answer is affirmative, the witness then points to biblical passages which outline the "plan of salvation": all are lost (Rom.
3:23); Christ died for our sins (John 3:16); confession of faith
brings salvation (Acts 2:38; 16:31).[30] After the plan has been
presented, the hearer is asked to make a verbal confession of
faith and join with the witness in prayer. Once a person says yes
to the plan of salvation approach, the witness assures him of
salvation. Thus, passive assent to the evangelist's scriptural quotations has replaced the frontier requirement of an open testimony, public examination, and evidence of an active, fruitful
Christian life.

The Anxious Inquirer

In 1844, R. Weiser defined a "mourner" as "one who, becoming alarmed about the state of his soul, began to pray and seek
deliverance from the bondage and dominion of sin."[31] The popu-
larity of instant evangelism rests upon its success with "anxious
inquirers." In the interviews used for this book, those who were
already anxious about their spiritual condition seemed to derive
the most immediate benefit from instant evangelism.[32] For example, a member of the administrative staff of a college was
asked to address the Young People's Sunday school department
of a local church. After his address, a high school girl asked to
see him. As they entered an empty classroom, she burst into
tears and said "I just *have* to help my mother!"

[30] This "plan" is more abbreviated than Crouch's. It is the type used by
students and pastors who presented instant evangelism interviews to the author.

[31] Quoted in McLindon, *op. cit.*, p. 1.

[32] It is hoped that this generalization, based on about two hundred cases, will
be checked by other investigators who will represent other denominations—
their theological or psychological points of view.

Mr. J: You have to help your mother?

Girl: Yes, she has such a hard time. You see my stepfather is un-saved and my mother is a Baptist.

Mr. J: And your mother needs help?

Girl: Yes, you see he doesn't like for her to go to church and he almost never goes himself. He just likes to run around and he thinks Mother should always sit at home. He doesn't let me come to church when he knows about it and Mother has almost quit coming because he doesn't like it. I just must help her (*still crying*).

Mr. J: How do you feel that you can help her?

Girl: Oh, I don't know (*pause*). If only I could do something, but I'm so weak.

Mr. J: So weak?

Girl: Yes—(*pause*)—Oh, Sir, I'm not even a Christian (*sobbing*).

Mr. J: You've never accepted Christ as Saviour?

Girl: Oh, no. God is so big and I'm so small. I've come to church for a long time and I know I should be a Christian but it just never seemed so important before.

Mr. J: Does it seem important to you now?

Girl (*stops crying and looks up*): Yes,—yes, it does.

Mr. J: (*takes New Testament out of shirt pocket*): Do you believe the Bible is God's Word to us?

Girl: Yes.

Mr. J: Would you like for us to read some Scripture verses concerning becoming a Christian?

At this point Mr. J read several passages (Rom. 3:23; 10:9; and others), explained briefly their meaning, and asked a few general questions to lead the girl to recognize herself as a sinner.

Mr. J: Would you like to pray and ask God to forgive you for your sins and save you?

Girl: I don't know how to pray to God—will you help me?

Mr. J: Certainly (*we bow our heads*). Would you like to tell God you're sorry for your sins and ask him to forgive you?

Girl: Yes. Oh, God, I *am* sorry for my sins, for being so weak and small. Please forgive me and help me to be strong. God, I believe in Jesus and love him and want him to be my Saviour. Help me, God, and help my mother. Amen.

Mr. J: Thank you, God, for Dot. Accept her prayer, give her strength and guidance as she begins her life with thee. Help her with her problem and show her what to do. Amen.

Girl (*looks up with a radiance in her face*): Oh, thank you. I feel

so *happy*. I know things will be all right now. Since Mother and I
are both Christians, we can work this out.

MR. J: Would you like to talk with your pastor now and tell him
what has happened?

GIRL: Yes, I would.

From this Dot and I went and talked with her pastor. He was glad to
hear about Dot's decision and said he was somewhat aware of the
problem in the home and would talk with Dot's mother and father
that afternoon if possible. Dot went forward at the morning service
to make public her profession of faith in Christ. I had to leave soon
after the morning service and have not heard any more from this.[33]

In his evaluation, Mr. J thought the interview went very well.
He admitted that the tears distressed him but that he was able to
draw Dot out some and help her to find peace with God. Yet,
at the same time, Mr. J had some doubts. What about the problem at home? Was it very great or was there something else that
she was hiding? What *really* made her so upset?

We do not know the answers to these questions because Mr. J
did not seek to understand her deeper strivings. When Dot said
that becoming a Christian was important, he was satisfied, and
reached for his Bible. *Why* was it so important? Instant evangelism wants to know only that the person is interested. Mr. J
pressed on for a decision. But after the decision, then what? How
would her profession of faith help Dot at home? She hinted
that it might be mother and Dot against stepfather. Did she seek
salvation for fear of her stepfather or in hope of protecting her
mother? Will Dot grow into a mature Christian? Has she had a
genuine conversion experience?

When this interview was presented to a group of pastors, some
asked if such questions were not irrelevant. After all, the girl had
professed faith! Is this not enough? In terms of the practice of
the early church and frontier American Christianity, the answer
is no. But times have changed. For example, in 1859 a Baptist
manual published in the South and one published in the North

[33] These and all other "verbatims" in the book are exact reproductions of the
material as it was handed to me by pastors and theological students. Only
names and places have been changed.

in 1903 required examination of the candidate.[34] But by 1951 a leading Southern Baptist authority in church administration pointed out that a candidate's fitness for church membership should be weighed, but "since the saving experience is essentially subjective, little objective evidence can be demanded." While a class for new members would be a good thing, any probation period might make good works a condition of salvation.[35]

Whatever decision a church may make about the manner of reception for members, there is one central question to be answered: has this individual entered a personal relationship with Christ?

In Dot's case, there was little understanding of the ways in which Christian faith would meet her specific needs. If her example is typical, then instant evangelism is defective, even when the inquirer is anxious. Dot wanted help. The witness was sincere in his desire to direct her toward Christ. But he did not take time to point her toward those personal paths that would illumine the deeper problems of her life with the abundant truth of the gospel.

A New Breath of Life

Does this mean that instant evangelism and the plan of salvation are all wrong? No, for there are countless persons who can testify that they began their Christian life through the kind of witness that has just been described. Furthermore, the Scripture passages recited in the "plan" are appropriate in themselves. The criticism is that they are being applied without reference to the personal needs of the inquirer and that instant evangelism is only *one* method of approach to unsaved persons. Unfortunately, it often has been taught and used as the only way of "soul-winning."

Instant evangelism needs to be unfettered by a new breath of life. The Spirit of God, that moves like the wind, cannot be contained in any one method. The necessity for a free spirit is high-

[34] Dagg, *op. cit.,* p. 269; Edward T. Hiscox, *The Standard Manual for Baptist Churches* (Philadelphia: Judson Press, 1903), pp. 23 ff.

[35] Gaines S. Dobbins, *The Churchbook* (Nashville: Broadman Press, 1951), p. 90.

lighted in the attempts of instant evangelists to deal with persons
who are *not* anxious about their salvation. Pastors who used this
rigid approach would repeat one Scripture verse after another in
a vain attempt to overcome spiritual resistance. Some ministers
threatened the hearer for not responding favorably. For example, one pastor said: "Well, you *know* that there's no hope for you
if you don't accept this word" (pointing to a certain Scripture
passage on man's sinfulness). When threatened, the recalcitrant
hearer would turn on the witness and defend his righteousness or
attack the hypocrisy of church members. The discussion soon became an argument.

In instant evangelism, a major problem is a lack of sensitivity
to the work of the Holy Spirit in human personality.

First, a witness may mistake his good intentions for the Holy
Spirit. For example:

Mrs. V. was visiting prospects for her sixteen-year-old girls' class.
She knocked on the door of a home in which she had never been,
and said: "I am Mrs. V, visiting from Central Church. Is Kay at
home?"

KAY: I'm Kay. Won't you come in?

MRS. V (*entering*): Thank you. (*They sit down.*) Kay, we are or-
ganizing a class for sixteen-year-old girls in our Sunday school. I'm
going to be teaching and we would love to have you visit with us
and perhaps even join us. (*Her response was a smile. I suggested
that she probably knew some of the girls who would be in the class
since they went to the same school. She said she knew one of
them.*) Do you attend church anywhere?

KAY: No. I used to go to church until my father started working on
Sundays. Now we don't go anywhere.

MRS. V: Are you a member of a church?

KAY: No, I'm not.

MRS. V: Have you ever thought about this matter?

KAY: No. I don't guess I have.

MRS. V: I'd like to read some Scriptures with you, Kay. (*We read
Rom. 3:23; 6:23; John 3:16, and I tried to explain these verses.
I tried to explain how Christianity really gives purpose to life and
enables one to know better what is right.*)

About this time Kay's mother came in and sat down and her sister
who had left soon after we started talking returned. I introduced my-

self to the mother and we talked a few minutes. I invited them all to our church and suggested that I could stop by for them if they did not have transportation. The mother said she guessed they were just too lazy to go but that she could take them if they wanted to go.

I left a copy of *Open Windows* and a tract with Kay and asked if I could come again, to which they replied yes.

Evaluation: I tried to kill two birds with one stone during this visit and made a terrible flop of both tries. Just a friendly visit to invite them to church would have been sufficient at this time and perhaps later followed up by an evangelistic visit. I knew too little about them to attempt any soul-winning.

Second, an evangelist may assume that by his own strength he, in a few minutes, can overcome entrenched resistance.

A new pastor was determined to "talk briefly" with Mr. N about the church. Mr. N is a seventy-five-year-old farmer who drinks openly, especially on weekends. The pastor walked out on the lot and after a few moments of general conversation said: "Mr. N, have you given much consideration to becoming a Christian?"

MR. N: No, I guess not.

PASTOR: Have you ever accepted Christ as your Saviour anytime in your life that you can recall?

MR. N: No, I don't guess I ever have.

PASTOR: You see a need in your life for becoming a Christian, don't you?

MR. N: Well, I've made it all right in life so far. My mother wasn't a church member either.

PASTOR: I'm sure that you realize that some day you will stand before God. (MR. N *remains silent.*) According to nature, God has blessed you by giving you a long life with pretty good health. Don't you think that the least that a person can do is to let God have his way in his life by believing in Christ as his Saviour?

MR. N: I guess so, but I don't want to today. (*Without saying another word, he turned and walked away, leading his mule toward the barn.*)

Evaluation: I could see that he had talked all he intended to that day, so I got in my car and drove home. Since that interview, I went back on a Sunday afternoon. Mr. N made his exit at the back door while his wife talked to me for a few minutes. From what I have been able to learn, this seems to be a true pattern of behavior for him. He seems to be allergic to all preachers or to anyone who makes inquiry about his spiritual condition.

Why is Mr. N allergic to Christian witnesses? Perhaps they, like this pastor, seek to create an immediate crisis in his life. Mr. N has learned how to reject that approach. Other persons guard themselves from pastors by silence, hurried exits, or exceptional politeness. In some cases the pastors may win them by patient attention. In other instances a dedicated layman may be the one who overcomes the resistance which a pastor cannot penetrate.

A third problem comes out of a neglect of the person's background. We do not know to what manner of person the Spirit may be speaking. Because the evangelist intensifies his interest on the present, he does not see the depths of personality. People appear as pictures pasted on cardboard. The interviews are flat and, for the moment, fleeting: When a pastor visited Mrs. G and asked if she were saved, she replied, "No, I've never had that feeling."

PASTOR: Feeling? I don't quite understand.
MRS. G: I don't know just how to say it, but it's that feeling you are supposed to have.
PASTOR: Do you have anything specific in mind?
MRS. G: No.
PASTOR: Do you have any idea what this feeling is supposed to be like?
MRS. G: No.
PASTOR: Then how would you know what it was if it came? (*The pastor then read John 3:16 to indicate that there is no mention of any type of "feeling." The woman shrugged her shoulders and soon changed the subject.*)

The interview was unsuccessful because the minister could see this woman only in a moment of time. If he had considered her as an individual with a history he would have recognized that she had received this idea about a "feeling" somewhere in the past. Was her background that of a group which emphasized a highly emotional experience? Was she plagued with some problem that led her to believe that an outpouring of "feeling" would bring relief? When these questions are considered, the individual can often supply his own answers.

Finally, the previous work of the Holy Spirit may be disregarded in instant evangelism. The witness is so concerned about what *he* is going to say that he does not ask what God may already have said to a man. There is an unthinking egotism in this. Like the medieval theologians who "dispensed grace" from Peter's "treasury of merit," some evangelists assume that in themselves they bring the Spirit to a visit.

We often miss this egotism in the rush of our godly words, as in the following:

Mr. C is slowly dying of cancer. His wife is anxious that he accept Christ before he dies. The pastor calls, and, after some preliminary conversation, pulls up a chair to Mr. C's bed.

PASTOR: Mr. C, I have been wanting to talk with you for some time about your relationship to Jesus Christ. Many times people put off considering what the Lord would have them do with their lives until it is too late to do anything about it. Would you like for me to talk with you about your relationship with the Saviour? (MR. C *indicates that he does.*) I would like to read a few passages from the Bible. Here we can find what God wants us to do with our lives. You do believe that in the Bible we can find what the right relationship between God and man is, don't you?

MR. C: Yes. I believe the Bible.

PASTOR: And you believe that Jesus is the Son of God and gave his life that we might be saved. (MR. C *nods his head.*) Do you believe that all men need to be saved? (MR. C *again indicates he does.*) Let me read just three passages of Scripture that tell us how to be saved. In the thirteenth chapter of Luke, the third verse, Jesus says, "Except ye repent, ye shall all . . . perish." By repenting, Jesus meant a turning from the old way of life to a new way of life. Do you think that men should repent of their sinful lives and turn to God? (MR. C *nods his head.*) If we repent of our sins, then, we should want to follow it up by doing what Christ would have us to do in order that we might be saved. (*Reads Rom. 10:9–10.*) Mr. C, doesn't this sound like the reasonable thing for all men to do?

MR. C: —Yes.

PASTOR: It isn't necessary for you to be in a church or before a group of people before you accept Christ as your Saviour. You can accept Christ as your Saviour right now if you want to. With Christ we can endure our suffering so much easier, because, if we will let him, he will take our burdens upon himself. But first we must let him. He will not force himself upon us. We read in Revelation 3:20: "Behold, I stand at the door, and knock: if any man hear my voice, and open the door, I will come in to him, and will sup with him, and he with me." Wouldn't you like to accept Christ as your Saviour now?

MR. C (*tries extremely hard to talk and finally gets out a few words*):
   I should;—but—I just can't give in.
PASTOR: Just ask him to save you and he will.
MR. C: Not now.

What is wrong? Surely the man knows his condition! The pastor has shown concern and has quoted Scripture passages on salvation. Why was he not touched? Mr. C did not respond because the pastor did not show an interest in the man's thoughts or the Spirit's work in his life. There may be other reasons for his resistance, but this one stands out. For months Mr. C had lain in bed. He was permitted to have few visitors. What did he think of all those days? Had he called upon God? Had God called to him? Would not most men, after all this suffering, have some thoughts of death? Yet the pastor was oblivious to these things. *He* brought the message of salvation.

The pastor may not be considered generally as overbearing or proud. In many areas of life he might be a humble, unassuming, sensitive person. But when he was "witnessing" he did not use his natural sensitivity to inquire into the stirrings of this man's heart.

Except with some anxious inquirers, instant evangelism has been found lacking. One by one, its assumptions and methods of evangelism have fallen short. Let us, therefore, turn to another type of witnessing and see how we may personally encounter people for Christ.

4

Personal Salvation

The previous chapters have probably raised more questions than they have provided answers. Many pastors may privately agree that they *ought* to give more time to those who are "growing up" into Christ, but *how?* It is difficult to sense the leading of the Spirit in a person's life. Recognition of the rich varieties of religious experience and the diagnosis of spiritual birth are exacting demands. With little training in pastoral counseling and less time for individual conferences, what is the average pastor to do?

The suggestions in this chapter are drawn from the interviews of "average" pastors. These were men who had little or no training in psychology before they entered a seminary course in pastoral care. Most of them were new in the pastorate, but the key to their interviews was the personal approach. The witnesses concentrated first upon the needs of the individuals with whom they talked. They first tried to find out what questions were paramount in the persons' minds. Then they sought to show how the Christian faith answered these needs. This approach made evangelism personal. It is the pastoral practice that is consistent with our presentation of a personal Saviour.

Jesus and the Samaritan Woman

Jesus' earthly ministry to the unawakened is the guiding spirit of personal evangelism. His conversation with the Samaritan woman is one of the most complete examples.[1] Christ's contact with this woman began with a simple human need—"Give

[1] Other examples of Jesus' forgiving companionship are given in H. R. Mackintosh, *The Christian Experience of Forgiveness* (London: James Nisbet & Co., 1927), chap. 4.

41

me a drink" (John 4:7). How natural his leading! How different from the greeting: "Are you saved?" or "Where will you spend eternity?"

The woman responded to this simple request by raising a question about Jesus' motivation: "Why did he talk to her, a Samaritan?" Had one of us been there, we might have answered our own needs by a long discourse on Jewish-Samaritan relations, or "why everybody must stay in his own place." But Jesus saw her need, a thirst for living water: "If you knew the gift of God, and who it is that is saying to you, 'Give me a drink,' you would have asked him, and he would have given you living water" (John 4:10).

The woman's curiosity then caused her to tell more about herself. Her materialistic and nationalistic mind was revealed in her answer: "Sir, you have nothing to draw with, and the well is deep; where do you get that living water? Are you greater than our father Jacob, who gave us the well, and drank from it himself, and his sons, and his cattle?" (John 4:11–12).

The Lord corrected her materialistic thinking by showing the contrast between her stone well and the eternal spring which he would create in a human life: "Every one who drinks of this water will thirst again, but whoever drinks of the water that I shall give him will never thirst; the water that I shall give him will become in him a spring of water welling up to eternal life" (John 4:13–14).

This was the woman's need—spiritual depth and perseverance. She rushed to accept it: "Sir, give me this water" (John 4:15). But her understanding was shallow. She responded to the deep appeal of Christ in terms of physical activity—"that I may not thirst, nor come here to draw" (John 4:15). Jesus did not equate physical activity with spiritual rebirth. Instead he began a spiritual diagnosis of this confused person by asking about her family: "Go, call your husband" (John 4:16).

The woman was evasive: "I have no husband" (John 4:17). Without rebuking her directly for this, Christ used her words to lay bare her marital failure—"he whom you now have is not your husband; this you said truly" (John 4:18). Shaken, the woman praised Jesus as a prophet and then sought to divert attention from herself by a nationalistic debate.

Jesus would not be diverted from her personal problem. He dealt briefly with her question and then concluded: "God is spirit, and those who worship him must worship in spirit and truth" (John 4:24). Again the woman was convicted. She had not been truthful. This man knew she had not. He had gently, yet firmly, shown her the gnawing needs of her own life. Could this be the Messiah? She could not say it straightforwardly, but indirectly she acknowledged him: "I know that Messiah is coming (he who is called Christ); when he comes, he will show us all things" (John 4:25). What she had obliquely stated, Jesus made direct and personal: "I who speak to you am he" (John 4:26).

This matchless dialogue reveals the patient concern of the Master for a personal conversion experience. His first concern was the woman's condition. He did not begin with a stylized plan of salvation but with a human request. He did not overcome her with superior arguments but intrigued her with answers to her deepest needs. Jesus revealed her to herself before he fully revealed himself to her as the Christ. The personal relationship was the medium for God's revelation.

How may we reverently enter into Christ's spirit in our approach to persons? The suggestions which follow provide a beginning. It is hoped that experienced pastors will go far beyond them. There are at least four elements in the personal approach to evangelism: (1) sensitivity to the previous history and background of a person; (2) awareness of the ways by which people relate to each other; (3) skill in personal conversation; and (4) the spiritual stature of the evangelist.

The Background of Personality

Every person has a history. An individual's background may contain events which have brought him to a dawning awareness of his need for Christ. Others may have suffered experiences in the past which are now roadblocks to faith.

When witnesses are sensitive to previous memories, they may

draw forth a rankling secret which has suppressed salvation. For example, a pastor reported his visit to a man who had been openly hostile to a former minister. During this pastoral call, the man brought out a picture album which contained snapshots from his youth. The pastor used this as an opportunity to ask about the man's early life. The man stated that he had gone to church with his mother when he was young but he now felt that the church "looked down on him" because he was drinking a good deal. The pastor replied that he knew that this kind of attitude must be very upsetting but showed that he also was interested in knowing how the man felt toward his drinking. The man gave a history of drinking that ended with the statement: "I have made so many promises to God that I do not believe he will ever accept me." The pastor said that the man probably had come to despise himself so much that he thought others would despise him, too. However, the pastor continued, God's evaluation is not the same as ours. God has cancelled our debts; he has nailed them to the cross, and through the cross has made a public example of the powers of sin and death that work within us.

This last comment, a paraphrase of Colossians 2:13–15, led to a discussion of Christian forgiveness and eventually into the man's surrender to Christ. Once the pastor had helped this man to speak of past experiences, his feelings could be related to the Christian faith in a way that brought personal conviction and commitment.

Sometimes a person will speak of a recent personal crisis. A sensitive evangelist can often lead from this to the question of commitment to Christ.

For example, a pastor called on a sixty-five-year-old man who was recently "shook up" by the death of his brother. Sensing his grief, the pastor quoted from the Sermon on the Mount: "Blessed are they that mourn for they shall be comforted."

After the old man had cried for a few minutes, he raised his head and said: "You know, Preacher, I am badly shook up by all this. It has made me begin to think about life after death."

The pastor asked if he wished to know about the provisions which God has made for our eternal life, thus opening a way to present the "plan of salvation." On the following Sunday morning the man made a public profession of his faith.

A person's understanding of conversion is conditioned by past expectations and present events. An intellectual explanation of salvation is not enough under these conditions. The evangelist must understand the previous history of the individual and the significant events that are related to religion. This may be illustrated in the conversation of a pastor with a woman who was waiting for the "feeling" of salvation:

> I visited Mrs. D on Saturday afternoon. This was the second time I had called. She is not a Christian. She is about fifty years of age. I seemed to get nowhere in leading her to a deeper commitment to Christ. On this occasion the husband was not at home. Three daughters were present. One, a retarded, crippled child remained in the room in a wheel chair. The other two daughters, who were older and married, remained in the kitchen preparing the evening meal. I knocked on the door and one of the daughters came to the door. She invited me in, and asked me to be seated and told me she would tell her mother I was there.
>
> MRS. D (*upon entering the room*): How are you, Brother Floyd? I'm glad to see you again.
> PASTOR: How are you, Mrs. D? I thought I would stop by and see if perhaps you wanted to continue our discussion since we were interrupted last time.
> MRS. D: All right. . . .
> PASTOR: The last time we talked, you told me you were very concerned about being a Christian and I believe that when we were interrupted we were talking about prayer.
> MRS. D: Yes, but I just don't have the feeling I ought to have.
> PASTOR: What kind of feeling do you think you should have?
> MRS. D: I don't know but I think I should feel differently.
> PASTOR: Have you ever heard others relate their experience of becoming a Christian?
> MRS. D: I'm not sure.
> PASTOR: I asked you this question because sometimes we expect our experiences to be a duplication of someone else's experiences and this is not always the case. Your experience may be a growing awareness of your need of God and of his presence.
> MRS. D: Yes, I think my experience may be different and entirely my own, but when I read the Bible there is just so much that I don't understand.

PASTOR: What are some of the things that puzzle you?

MRS. D: Just so much of the Bible.

PASTOR: Is it the Bible that puzzles you or are you confused about things that have happened in your life?

MRS. D: Do you mean about Susie and all?

PASTOR: Yes, do you have any questions in your mind about the justice of this or why God might have allowed it to happen?

MRS. D: No, I am not bitter. I do not blame God. I know this has happened to a lot of people. It is just one of those crosses we have to bear.

PASTOR: Mrs. D, I have found in my own life that trying circumstances of life make us better people. They draw us nearer to God.

MRS. D: Yes, I know that is true.

PASTOR: Mrs. D, you told me that you had prayed. Was there any indication that God answered your prayers at any time?

MRS. D: No, I don't think so.

PASTOR: You mean that nothing whatever happened to make you think that perhaps God had heard and was answering your prayer?

MRS. D: I remember once when I was in the hospital and facing an operation. I prayed for God to help me through the operation and to help me not to be afraid. I remember that I was no longer afraid and I told my roommate that I had prayed and how differently I felt. I was no longer afraid. You know, it was remarkable how differently I felt and how calm I was all the rest of the time before my operation.

PASTOR: Then don't you believe that God answered your prayer? You received help from somewhere to overcome your fear.

MRS. D: Yes, he did. (*At this point her countenance seemed to brighten as if she had developed a new insight.*)

PASTOR: Mrs. D, did you make any promises to God when you asked him to help you?

MRS. D: Yes, I promised him that I'd be a better person and that I'd live a better life. (*At this point the husband entered and our trend of conversation was interrupted.*)

Pastor's evaluation: I feel that I made some progress in this interview.

First, I think some progress was made in correcting a misunderstanding about what kind of feeling a person should have as a Christian. I later learned from the husband that the children used to attend a Holiness Church where much stress was placed on emotionalism. This is perhaps where she got the impression that she was to have a certain kind of feeling. The Holiness pastor had visited in the home on several occasions and had talked with the family.

Second, I think the air was cleared as far as any question in my mind about the retarded child. I believe at this point I was able to identify myself with her as a person who knows something about trials and sorrows of life although mine are not the same as hers. I think she appreciated this.

Third, I believe I helped her to see that God is concerned about her and that she has every reason to believe that she has experienced answered prayer. I believe I should have allowed her to talk more at the point where she said she was confused when reading the Bible. I think she is having real trouble here.

The pastor has seen the influence of another type of religious experience and the interpretation of suffering upon Mrs. D's struggle toward God. It may be some time before this will be clear to Mrs. D. By referring again to her understanding of the Bible and her interpretation of suffering, he may lead her to a better knowledge of God's ways with men.

Unfortunately, some pastors do not seem to realize that people have a history. They tend to deal with issues of a personal nature as though they exist only today. As a result, people appear to them as flat images without depth. It may be that these pastors are superficial because they are repressing the memories of their own past. If, like Augustine, they would plunge into the depths of memory, they might find both themselves and God. Perhaps through the cultivation of deeper strata of their own personality they would learn how to prepare the soul of another for the reception of God's grace.

In the parable of the sower Jesus showed that the condition of the soul would affect the reception of the gospel. The Word of God may fall upon stony, hard-packed, or shallow soil. The servants of Christ must know how to unearth obstacles which are buried like hard rock in personality. They must learn how to venture beyond the beaten paths of a person's resistance into the more receptive areas of individual need. The gospel must be firmly rooted to the past memories, present needs, and future hopes of those to whom we witness.

Sensitivity in Personal Relationships

Christian truth is imparted through saved personalities. The Spirit of God chose to witness to men through men (2 Cor.

5:18–21). The Word is alive when carried through a deep personal relationship from the evangelist to the hearer. Here is one example. A young pastor was told: "Every preacher has worked on Mr. C and no one has ever been able to move him." The pastor found that Mr. C's wife was a Christian but had never moved her membership to a local church. He also discovered that a number of preachers had sought out Mr. C as though he were the greatest sinner in the community and had belabored him with many warnings about his condition.

The pastor decided that he would not push the man too hard. His first desire was to get to know Mr. and Mrs. C. This was not hard to do, since both of them occasionally attended his church. One Sunday, Mr. C invited the pastor to visit him, which the pastor did. Mr. C began to come to church more often as the pastor continued to visit him. After about six months, the pastor saw the first desire of the man to talk about religion.

"Preacher, I wonder why you have never talked to me about becoming a Christian?" The pastor hesitated, and before he could answer, Mr. C continued, "I have always wanted my wife and children to go to church. It is the best thing in the world for them. As for me, I have lived better than most of the people in the church. I can go to heaven on my own moral life."

The pastor replied, "Mr. C, you have always been a good man in my eyes, but the Bible says that all men are sinners before God. Paul teaches us that no man is righteous in God's sight. I enjoy your company very much, but I must honestly say that unless a man repents of his sins and accepts Christ as personal Saviour, he can never be justified before God." Mr. C became very angry and said he did not want to talk about that subject any more.

After this conversation Mr. C came to church no more. His wife continued to come and reported that her husband was still angry. When the pastor asked why she had never joined the church, she replied, "I like this church, but I want to leave my membership where I was baptized."

Several weeks later the pastor talked with Mrs. C about becoming a member of his church. He explained, "Mrs. C, I know that you are troubled about your husband's reluctance to join the church. Would it be possible that you have not been the right kind of witness yourself?"

At this, Mrs. C said, "Well, Preacher, since you put it that way, I guess you are right. If I am going to move my husband, I guess I will have to move myself."

The pastor did not know what happened between then and Sunday, but at the morning worship service Mrs. C stepped forward on the first stanza of the invitational hymn. Her husband was only a few steps behind her. He confessed Christ and was baptized.

This example presents two kinds of relationships which are important in personal evangelism. First, there is the bond that has been created between the pastor and Mr. C through repeated visits and conversations. The pastor did not push Mr. C as he had expected to be pushed. Instead, the minister waited patiently for Mr. C to introduce the subject of salvation. Because he had dealt with this man for six months, he was able to state frankly his biblical principles of salvation. Although the man was angry enough to cease church attendance for a time, it seems from his subsequent actions that his nonattendance provided a "cooling off" period.

Second, the pastor was also sensitive to the relationship between husband and wife. It gradually dawned on him that the wife's indecision was a key to the husband's lack of commitment. Therefore, when the husband withdrew from him, he was able to continue his witness through the wife. As a result, both were won to the church.

Despite the importance of family ties, some pastors have yet to become aware of the way in which one member of the family is different from another. One pastor visited a man who had just suffered a serious illness. When he began to ask questions about the man's spiritual welfare, the wife became very protective of her husband and began to make excuses for him. The pastor's attention was diverted by the wife's chatter and he did not center his attention upon the man again. If he had been sensitive to the relationship of these people to each other and to him, he might have asked himself: "Why was this woman so quick to answer for him?"

In summary, the evangelist must be sensitive to the bond between family members and his own personal impact upon those to whom he witnesses. Some pastors have little awareness that their feelings are important to people. As a result, their spiritual conversations carry no warmth. For example, Mr. X had stated to his pastor that he was lost and would appreciate prayer. Since the pastor did not think he was the type of person that could be led quickly into a decision, the pastor called on him a second time:

PASTOR: I have been praying for you as you asked me to do.
MR. X: I appreciate your interest, Preacher.
PASTOR: Well, are you ready to accept Christ and believe in him as your personal Saviour?

Mr. X looked surprised for a moment and then stated that he was not quite sure. The pastor immediately plied him with many scriptural passages about his need for salvation. Throughout his conversation, there was no word of appreciation for the man's interest in salvation nor a concern for the problems and objections which he raised. The pastor took it for granted that Mr. X knew that the pastor was glad to see his interest. But this joy was never shown.

In contrast, another pastor sought out an unsaved man for conversation whenever he was in the village store. He would "drop by" and pay him a brief visit from time to time. After several weeks, the man confided that the church members probably considered him "a hardened sinner." When the pastor asked why this was so, he replied: "Well, I had a run-in with one of the former Sunday school superintendents about the way in which we did some things. I have not been back to the church since. Of course, I am not much of a man to criticize others, since I have never professed religion myself."

The pastor then made clear his deep interest for this man's salvation: "Brother Johnson, I have longed to speak to you about your spiritual condition, but we were either in the presence of other people or in too much of a hurry to discuss these deep things. I am so happy that you have given me this opportunity." Tears came into Mr. Johnson's eyes as he said: "I believe you, Preacher." The pastor then used biblical quotations to instruct Mr. Johnson in the Christian way of life. The Word was alive because Mr. Johnson was convinced of his pastor's personal love for him.

Skill in Personal Conversation

Personal graciousness is a part of the Christian doctrine of God's grace. Jesus admonished his disciples to savor their conversation, to season their words even as salt mellows and brings out the rich flavor of food. The ability to speak the right word, to catch a meaningful phrase, is an invaluable aid in evangelism. The words of the Bible are the most gracious and precious in our Christian heritage. In personal evangelism the pastor imparts this spirit in his conversations with others.

A number of pastors show exceptional ability to follow a person's meaning and encourage him to speak of spiritual things. This is an art which is given to some and learned by others. Here is one example. A pastor was visiting in a home when the wife volunteered the information that she was a Baptist. The pastor expressed his pleasure at knowing this, continued his conversation with her for a few moments, and then turned to the husband.

PASTOR: Mr. J, are you a member of the First Church also?
MR. J: No, I am not a member of any church.
PASTOR: Have you ever thought about becoming a member or have you thought a great deal about your spiritual needs?
MR. J: Yes, I have.
PASTOR: Have you been thinking about this lately?
MR. J: More than ever before.
PASTOR: What has been your experience in facing your spiritual needs in the past?

Mr. J then described some of his personal experiences with preachers and his knowledge of what the gospel is.

The pastor had graciously led the conversation about the church from the wife to the husband. He had asked the type of questions that would allow Mr. J to give favorable responses. He did not embarrass him by unfavorable comparisons to his wife, such as: "Don't you think that you ought to join the church with your wife?" Essentially, the pastor was showing his faith in Mr. J by assuming that he may have thought something about becoming a Christian to meet his spiritual needs.

Some pastors are also able to help people understand the issues of life. They clarify some of the cloudy problems that stand in the way of an individual's spiritual pilgrimage. One evangelist capably led an unsaved person in the following manner:

MR. B: You keep pointing out in the Bible that Jesus called me to a committal of my life to him. It keeps coming out that a committal of life is what salvation really is. Right?

PASTOR: Have these observations seemed correct to you?

MR. B: Well, yes, they have, but I don't know. My life has not been committed to Christ. I have continued doing as I please.

PASTOR: Are you satisfied with this type of life?

MR. B: I was, but somehow what you have said and the witness of some of the members of my Sunday school class have not made me so sure. I don't do too many real bad things, but I have certainly never made Jesus the ruling factor in my life.

PASTOR: And now you are considering this?

Mr. B then made a positive statement about his desire to know how the Christian faith would be related to his own personal experiences. The pastor did not enter into an intellectual debate about the merits of commitment to Christ. Mr. B was already fully informed about that. What was now necessary was an opportunity for him to express the stirrings of his own soul.

It is difficult for some pastors to lead people out in the way that has just been described. In one study, a number complained that they could not get any personal commitment from those to whom they talked. Sometimes the difficulty became evident when the pastor was persuaded to write up the interview. For example, a man admitted to his pastor that he had done much evil. The pastor repeated many verses from Romans on the reality of sin and the necessity for forgiveness. The man became very quiet and had nothing more to say. The pastor had "run over him" with the Scriptures rather than listening to the heartfelt need of this penitent. If the witness had graciously inquired as to how the man felt now about his sins, the person might have been encouraged to speak of his spiritual need.

Some ministers seem to have little tolerance for feelings which are disagreeable to them. Hostile or depressed emotions are immediately rejected. Persons are expected to become kind and hopeful right away. If not, the pastor abandons them. This swift reaction indicates that the pastor cannot tolerate such feelings in himself. When he is depressed, he immediately overlays it with "positive thoughts." When hostile, he is so alarmed that he denies the very thought that overwhelms him. As a result, psychologists have found that ministers turn hostility in upon themselves, become depressed, and are unusually sensitive to criticism.[2]

To improve his relationships, a pastor might ask himself, "How do *I* react to disappointment?" "What emotions arise in me when I am frustrated?" He may also ask someone whom he respects to give him an unvarnished answer to these questions. "How do others see me?" is as important as "How do I see myself?" From an examination of these two questions the evangelist may find some valuable leads to the question: "Why do I react this way to the feelings of others?"

Another test of conversational skill is the well-timed use of appropriate Scripture material. One pastor sensed a person's need and presented a helpful verse of Scripture. A young mother had said: "I worry a great deal about my life, my marriage, and my home." As the pastor asked about the causes of worry, he found few objective reasons for her disturbance. Finally, the woman said: "I guess that most of it is in me. I—I need something greater than myself, something to live for. But I feel so unworthy."

[2] Some evidence of this is published in Harold Massey's "Apperception Tests Reveal Ministerial Students' Attitudes," *The Southern Baptist Educator*, April, 1957.

The pastor wrote in his summary of the interview: "I felt that she needed assurance that God would hear her despite her feeling of unworthiness." So he opened his Bible to the first letter of John and read: "If we confess our sins, he is faithful and just, and will forgive our sins and cleanse us from all unrighteousness" (1 John 1:9).

After several remarks of interpretation and support, she left the study, expressing a sense of real relief. The pastor continued to think of her, for her problems were obviously not yet solved. On the following Sunday, she came forward on confession of faith. In the following months she found a place of acceptance in the church as one of their best Sunday school teachers. The Scripture verse in itself did not produce these results. But its use at the right time helped to seal the sense of God's acceptance and forgiveness which this woman felt.

Biblical quotations reveal the pastor's ability to see the relevance of the gospel to personal life. The pastor who ponders the Scriptures and reflects on their meaning for his life will be spontaneous in his quotations. The written Word has become a living Word in him. His cultivation of a loving and open spirit toward others will increase his sensitivity to personal need. The Spirit of the Scriptures and the words of the Scriptures will harmonize in his conversation.

There is no substitute for this careful cultivation of the Spirit. Pastors should not be content with mechanical schemes that present a sinner's argument and a Scripture verse that defeats it. The Bible is not a system of isolated propositions with which an argument may be won. It is the revelation of God's mighty acts in human personality.

The Pastor's Maturity

The discerning use of the Scriptures and flexibility in conversation are closely related to the pastor's personal maturity. The pastor who has gained a mature acceptance of his own feelings is better able to hear and handle the difficult emotions of others.

A crucial problem in spiritual maturity is the question of humility. The mature pastor rejoices in the initiative which a person takes toward God. He encourages the individual to formulate his own answers to the great questions of life. He is pleased that the convert can anticipate thoughts which the pastor might have. This spirit of humility is reflected in the following portion of an interview between a pastor and a woman who had lost a child.

PASTOR: You seem to be saying that in avoiding looking at yourself, at your religious convictions, some things have been lost along the way and now you want to find them, or look for them.

MRS. MC (*long pause*): You know, I've never said it, but I don't believe the church meant very much to me (*chuckle*). I never came alive until I married. Oh, how I've enjoyed my marriage (*smiling*). But I never realized until this happened that we both left something out.

PASTOR: God?

MRS. MC (*smiles*): I'm glad you said it. What do you think I should do?

PASTOR: Well, I'd hate to suggest any hard and fast rule, but I would suggest you might do something you haven't done before.

MRS. MC: Go to church?

PASTOR: No, that's not exactly it; I was thinking of something you said earlier. I got the impression that—

MRS. MC: I could talk to my husband (*smiling*). Not once have we done that! I think it would be a relief to both of us to bring this out in the open (*long pause*). When you first came in I thought you were going to preach me a sermon about not worrying about my child (*laughing*).

PASTOR: Looks like you stole my thunder.

MRS. MC: I hate not having my child, but don't you think God's taking care of him? (PASTOR *nods*.) I can't wait until my husband comes tonight. I'm going to bring it up. I hope he suggests talking to you. I do appreciate all you've told me.

PASTOR: I'd be glad to talk with you if you like.

MRS. MC: He's not coming until after supper. We'll let you know.

PASTOR: That will be fine. If you'd like, why don't we share our conversation with God in a prayer together. (MRS. MC *nods*.) "We acknowledge thee, our Father, as our Lord. We place ourselves and those whom we love in thy care. We place our loved ones whom we have lost in thy mercy. As we face now crucial decisions, grant unto us the guidance of the Holy Spirit. In Jesus' name, amen."

The pastor became God's representative in the communication of feeling. How different this spirit is from that of pastors who are so eager to give their own answers that they have no time to rejoice at the answers of others. This is very disheartening to the layman who may have struggled for weeks to formulate some solution to the needs of his life. He thinks God has revealed something to him but the pastor brushes it aside with: "Oh, the apostle Paul put it much better two thousand years ago when he said. . . ."

If the sinner does not submit to the immature pastor's argument, then he is rebuked and threatened. When a recalcitrant person argues, the minister insists that he is right; in fact, he may marshal an impressive array of scriptural texts to prove his point. At no time does he stop to inquire into the work which God may already have accomplished in this person's life.[3]

The Dangers of Personal Evangelism

Personal evangelism requires careful and reverent attention to the background of a person and his relationship to the pastor and other persons. A pastor needs skill in personal conversation and spiritual maturity. Yet none of these qualities by itself, nor all of them together, can provide an adequate answer to evangelism. In fact, the personal approach to evangelism is especially treacherous because words like "personality," "interpersonal," "relationship," and "communication" are so popular today. It is all too easy to equate modern psychological techniques with successful soul-winning.

The major danger of personal evangelism is humanism—the substitution of human moods for the Spirit of God. The suggestions of this chapter may degenerate into an emphasis on good feelings between persons. The great Person of salvation, Jesus Christ, may be neglected. An example of this problem may be seen in the following interview of a pastor with a woman who had been an alcoholic. The pastor skilfully led her to tell how the church and Alcoholics Anonymous had helped her regain

[3] Consider Paul's discussion of a humble ministry in 2 Corinthians 4:7–15, 1 Corinthians 1:18–31.

sobriety. Reaching a deeper level, the woman discussed her first marriage as a contributing factor to her drinking. Her recent marriage to a man whom she met at an AA meeting was a stabilizing influence. She now felt that her life was different:

PASTOR: And now life is so different?

MRS. A: Yes. It's funny how it can happen. You can be fouled up and six months later be so completely happy. That's why I say I'm the happiest person.

PASTOR: This is really conversion for you?

MRS. A: Yes, that's about it.

PASTOR (*after pause*): I must say, I've enjoyed talking with you about these things.

The interview concluded with good wishes and prayer. In terms of psychological "adjustment," this was a good interview. But when the goals of conversion are introduced, it must be judged a failure. At a crucial moment the pastor backed away from the spiritual significance of her new happiness.

Personal evangelism, therefore, must be more than "personal." It must move through the needs of individuals to the place where they are confronted by the person of Christ. One facet of our work is the incarnation of God's Spirit in human personality. Our lives, our attitudes, are his witness. But the other facet is of equal importance.

There must be an open confrontation of Jesus. Our Lord led the Samaritan woman to the place where she would ask the right questions; then he directly became her personal answer. We can listen and lead also; there are problems to be identified, attitudes to be clarified, long-dormant emotions to be awakened. But above all, there is a Saviour to be glorified. It is our high privilege to minister so personally to individuals that they will meet Christ face to face.

5

A Pastoral Theology
of Evangelism

In his discussion of reconciliation, John Oman asked this question: "How otherwise than by finding what life signifies for personal relations is life ever transformed?" [1] The transforming power of Christ rests upon the revelation of God in human flesh. This incarnational theology begins in the person of Jesus and is continued in the life of every believer. Evangelism that is true to a personal Saviour must know the meaning of Christian doctrine in life experience. The witness who "gets down to cases" will see personal relations as a channel of Christian revelation. This is theology from a pastoral viewpoint.

The Reformation began with such an emphasis in pastoral theology. Melanchthon, Gerhard, and others made an intense study of the psychology of conversion.[2] Puritans like Doddridge described the personal impact of guilt, sin, and redemption.[3] The most popular Baptist work, *The Pilgrim's Progress,* presented in living drama the process of salvation. This sixteenth- and seventeenth-century interest in the personal aspects of conversion was not sustained in eighteenth-century theology. "Classical" theologians arranged the propositions of orthodoxy into statements that said much about God's action and little about man's response. By 1861, Heinrich Heppe had organized the Calvinistic propositions into twenty-eight categories in *Re-*

[1] John Oman, *Grace and Personality* (New York: Association Press, 1961), p. 105.
[2] Paterson, *op. cit.,* pp. 105 ff.
[3] Philip Doddridge, *Rise and Progress of Religion in the Soul* (New York: D. Appleton & Co., 1835).

formed Dogmatics and buttressed them with quotations from sixteenth- to nineteenth-century theologians. Conversion was treated as a series of affirmations about God's dealing with the elect.[4]

These "classical" treatises showed little concern for the personal relations by which conversion might be accomplished. Furthermore, human sensibilities were offended by dogmatic assertions about the damnation of infants and the vengeance of God through human suffering.

An answer to this unappealing system appeared in the mid-nineteenth century. It was Horace Bushnell's *Christian Nurture*. The work showed a sensitive concern for children and parents. It contained numerous practical suggestions and applications of theological principles. Bushnell elevated family relations as an instrument of regeneration and rejected the Calvinistic theory that the family was a vehicle of depravity.[5]

In an extreme reaction against the doctrines and practices of his day, Bushnell completely rejected any crisis experience in conversion. This approach became the rallying point for a new, liberal outlook in theology. The successors of Bushnell moved boldly into social and political applications of their faith. In reaction to this, conservative theologians retreated into renewed affirmations of orthodoxy. Personal implications of conversion were reduced to individual works of piety, churchly practices, and the avoidance of "worldliness."[6] "The Gospel was often narrowed to personal and pietistic religious experience, in which the spiritual role of the intellect is disparaged, and the social and cultural imperative of Christianity evaded."[7]

By the opening of the twentieth century, Episcopal, Lutheran, and Presbyterian divines stressed nurture and religious develop-

---

[4] Heinrich Heppe, *Reformed Dogmatics* (London: George Allen & Unwin, 1950), pp. 510–42.

[5] Horace Bushnell, *Christian Nurture* (New Haven: Yale University Press, 1948), pp. 91–94.

[6] See W. M. Horton, "Systematic Theology" in Arnold Nash (ed.), *Protestant Thought in the Twentieth Century: Whence and Whether?* (New York: The Macmillan Co., 1951), pp. 105–11.

[7] C. F. H. Henry, *Evangelical Responsibility in Contemporary Theology* (Grand Rapids: Wm. B. Eerdmans Publishing Co., 1953), p. 46.

ment in the tradition of Bushnell. Baptists and Methodists tended to retain the frontier emphasis upon the necessity of a conversion experience.[8] The former group wrote formal treatises on the pastoral office while the latter prepared practical manuals for successful revivals. Pastoral theology became a series of exhortations illuminated by personal anecdotes.

In the absence of theological inquiry, questions about personal evangelism were investigated by psychologists: Edwin Starbuck, J. H. Leuba, G. Stanley Hall, Irving King, E. S. Ames, George Coe, E. T. Clark, William James. Their quest for scientific objectivity led them away from the conscious acknowledgment of theological presuppositions. By the 1930's pastors were faced with an unenviable choice. They might read systematic theologies that majored on doctrinal propositions, or they could turn to studies of personal conversion that contained no affirmations of faith. "Orthodox" systematic theologies contained the substance of salvation in dogmatics, while "objective" psychologists presented the meaning of salvation in human life.

This cleavage has not yet been completely repaired. Modern systematic theologians give slight attention to the signs of conviction in man's consciousness or the interpersonal aspects of conversion. In fact, systematic theologians make few references of any kind to evangelism or conversion. Only by picking and choosing that which is relevant, a student may find sections in major works that will be of value for the theology of evangelism. Some representative examples may be found in Barth, Brunner, Bultmann, and Niebuhr.

The emphasis of Karl Barth is upon the decision of God to save depraved men. Conversion is a decisive awakening.[9] This is a needed emphasis which has such practical application as Barth's insistence upon believer's baptism.[10] But unfortunately for evangelism, Barth retains an extreme emphasis on the depravity of human nature. As the Lutheran theologian, T. A. Kan-

---

[8] Seward Hiltner, "Pastoral Theology," in Nash, *op. cit.*, p. 181.

[9] Karl Barth, *Church Dogmatics* (New York: Charles Scribner's Sons, 1955), IV, 553-83.

[10] *The Teaching of the Church Regarding Baptism* (London: SCM Press, 1954).

tonen puts it: "If natural man has no capacity to hear the Word of God, and God arbitrarily saves whom He will, there is little incentive to preach the Word." [11] Because Barth's theology is organized about the acts of God, his systematic volumes contain less material on the meaning or manner of man's response than may be found in his published sermons.

Emil Brunner has more concern for the response of man but a less clearly defined statement on conversion than Barth. Brunner maintains that man has been created by God for free, spontaneous self-determination. This freedom must be used responsibly. To do this, the marred image of God in man must be restored by a leap of faith in Christ. This brings the new birth, a state and process "in which man no longer strains after God but receives his life and strength from God." [12] The aim of modern theology has been to show absolute identity between ethics and faith.

Brunner's major contribution is in the social and ethical implications of Christian faith, the redemption of the "orders" of society. As in Barth's dogmatics, individual and interpersonal aspects of salvation receive scant attention in Brunner's systematic or social works. For example, spiritual rebirth is affirmed as a necessity in the transformation of an unjust man but there is no description of the personal process by which this "conversion" takes place.[13] His evangelistic emphasis is to be found in sermons such as "The Great Invitation."

Rudolf Bultmann stresses surrender and commitment in conversion. All human accomplishment and boasting are under God's condemnation. Those who repent of their pride enter a new self-understanding in which life is lived from God as center. There must be continual surrender of self in obedient sub-

---

[11] T. A. Kantonen, *The Theology of Evangelism* (Philadelphia: Muhlenberg Press, 1954), p. 36.

[12] Emil Brunner, *The Divine Imperative* (Philadelphia: The Westminster Press, 1947), p. 159; *The Christian Doctrine of Creation and Redemption* (Philadelphia: The Westminster Press, 1952), pp. 55–61; *The Mediator* (Philadelphia: The Westminster Press, 1947), pp. 592 ff.

[13] ———, *Justice and the Social Order* (New York: Harper & Brothers, 1945), pp. 259–61.

mission to the judgment of God made known in the cross of Christ.[14] But a personal relation to Christ is rejected by Bultmann as "foreign to the earliest Christian message."

Reinhold Niebuhr shares Bultmann's emphasis upon the sin of pride. In Niebuhr's writing, it is not sin to be a human being. Sin is the denial of humanity, the attempt to be more than human (pride) or less than human (sensuality). When man finds that he cannot will the good, the mediation of Christ moves him from despair to repentance, from repentance to hope. The old self is shattered and Christian experience brings a new selfhood. The Christian man lives by grace, a power not his own, that continually offers pardon for recurring pride.[15]

Niebuhr is the major modern theologian who relates the doctrines of sin and grace to the human self. But although there are eloquent applications to the social scene, Niebuhr's books contain no discussion of conversion.[16] Niebuhr is so concerned with social issues that the acceptance of racial equality is more important to him than a clear distinction between "saved" and "unsaved" persons.[17] He believes that Christians should accept the religion of the Jews and not break down ethnic and religious separateness. This latter comment in the 1958 *Journal of the Central Conference of American Rabbis* brought Niebuhr under strong attack from George Sweazey. To Sweazey, Niebuhr's (and Tillich's) refusal to include the Jews in evangelism strikes at the very heart of the gospel witness.[18]

If the evangelistic witness is not maintained by modern systematic theologians, where may it be found? There are trends in theology that provide a partial answer. The first is the writing of "orthodox" theologians such as C. F. H. Henry of *Christianity*

---

[14] Rudolf Bultmann, *The Theology of the New Testament* (New York: Charles Scribner's Sons, 1951), pp. 73, 89, 187–88, 286 ff.

[15] Reinhold Niebuhr, *The Nature and Destiny of Man* (New York: Charles Scribner's Sons, 1941), I, 178–240; II, 98–126.

[16] See, for example, the one paragraph allusion to salvation in Reinhold Niebuhr's *The Self and the Dramas of History* (New York: Charles Scribner's Sons, 1955), p. 66.

[17] Reinhold Niebuhr, "Literalism, Individualism and Billy Graham," *The Christian Century*, May 23, 1956, p. 642.

[18] George Sweazey, "Are Jews Intended to Be Christians?" *The Christian Century*, April 29, 1959, p. 514.

Today and E. J. Carnell of Fuller Theological Seminary. In his *Christian Commitment,* Carnell presents a lengthy and personally relevant section on guilt and sin as precursors of conversion. But the next section of the book contains no elaboration on conversion, the new birth, or the meaning of a redeemed life. C. F. H. Henry has included in *Christian Personal Ethics* a chapter on "Christian Ethics as the Morality of the Regenerate Man." Only when man is "born again" does the life of moral virtue move toward Godlikeness. This is a biblically-centered interpretation of the new birth as a central condition of Christian morality. Unfortunately, neither Henry nor Carnell presents the pastoral aspects of conversion.

A second theological trend has been named "biblical theology." In this area there are excellent works on specialized aspects of salvation. A. M. Hunter has organized Pauline theology as salvation—past, present, and future.[19] Vincent Taylor has provided an exegesis of the New Testament meanings of conversion and related terms in *Forgiveness and Reconciliation.*[20] James Stewart presents reconciliation and justification as aspects of Paul's central phrase "a man in Christ."[21] The redemptive work of Christ is the subject of D. M. Baillie's *God Was in Christ.*

These biblical monographs have replaced systematic works as a major source of theological information on conversion. This is a new development. A few years ago, the systematic theologies of Charles Hodge, A. H. Strong, E. Y. Mullins, and W. T. Conner contained extensive references to conversion.[22] Today, a systematic treatment of evangelism would be found only in a specialized book on that subject. Some of the best examples of this are Culbert Rutenber's *The Reconciling Gospel;* Daniel T. Niles' *That They May Have Life;* World Council of Churches' "Theological

[19] Hunter, *Interpreting Paul's Gospel, op. cit.*

[20] See also his *Atonement in the New Testament Teaching* (Napierville, Ill.: Alec R. Allenson, Inc., 1954).

[21] *A Man in Christ* (New York: Harper & Brothers, 1935).

[22] Hodge, *Systematic Theology* (New York: Charles Scribner's Sons, 1898); Strong, *Systematic Theology* (New York: Press of E. R. Andrews, 1886); Mullins, *The Christian Religion in Its Doctrinal Expression, op. cit.;* Conner, *op. cit.*

Reflection on the Work of Evangelism"; and T. A. Kantonen's *The Theology of Evangelism*. Rutenber's volume, prepared for American Baptist laymen, is a presentation of the divine gospel and the human response in readable, personal terms.

In pastoral theology, the relationship of saving grace to personal response may be seen in many ways. Each evangelist needs to see how other people interpret doctrine and how doctrine may be applied to individual needs. In the material that follows, some specific issues of faith will be related to the pastoral interviews of an evangelist. These are some starting points for a pastoral theology of evangelism.

Separation from God

The threshold of saving grace is a person's awareness of his need for a Saviour. It may be described as a need for deliverance from physical illness (Matt. 9:21), danger (Matt. 8:25), life's infection (Acts 2:40), lostness (Matt. 18:11), sin (Matt. 1:21), wrath (Rom. 5:9), judgment (Rev. 20:12).[23] Looking within, a person may see the dominion of human desire as the cause of a gulf toward God: "We all once lived in the passions of our flesh, following the desires of body and mind . . ." (Eph. 2:3).

How do people feel this separation from God, this lostness? For some, the violation of religious taboos is thought to be the major barrier to God. For example, Pastor M visited Mrs. R:

MRS. R: Hello, Brother M., I'm glad to see you again. I guess you have wondered why we haven't been to church?

PASTOR: Yes, I had hoped to see you in our services.

MRS. R: Well, my husband works nights and usually we go out on Saturday night and do not get in until late and are not able to get up and go to church. I know we ought to go for the children's sake, if not for our own, but we think very little about it until Ray or Paul stops by to talk to us about it.

PASTOR: You appreciate their interest in you?

MRS. R: Yes, we do very much, but I think there are some things I am just not ready to give up in order to become a Christian.

PASTOR: What is it that you are not willing to give up?

[23] William Barclay, *A New Testament Wordbook* (New York: Harper & Brothers, 1955), pp. 119–21.

Mrs. R: Well, smoking for one thing. I am just not ready to quit. (*She had just lit a cigarette.*)

Pastor: You feel that you would have to quit smoking to be a Christian?

Mrs. R: I definitely do. I don't think you can be a Christian and smoke and go to card parties and drink. Now I drink socially. We attend parties and everyone drinks and I do too, just to be sociable. That's the only reason I drink. (Mrs. R *sends the boys to their room to play.*)

Pastor: Why do you feel that a Christian cannot smoke or play cards?

Mrs. R: Well, my mother is a member of the ——— church and they believe that a Christian cannot do any of those things, even wear lipstick.

Pastor: Does the Bible say that a Christian cannot smoke?

Mrs. R: I guess it does; I don't know. Does it?

Pastor: No. The Bible says nothing about smoking as such. There are some things you do not have a yes or no answer for in the Bible. Some things you have to decide for yourself on the basis of principles found in the Bible.

Mrs. R: Well, as I said, we attend parties and all of our friends drink and I don't think I'm ready to leave all of our friends. They are the only people we know here.

Pastor: Do you have to drink because they do?

Mrs. R: If you want to have any fun you do.

Pastor: You feel you would have no fun if you were a Christian?

Mrs. R: I can't see any fun in just singing and praying and going to church. I know that you enjoy those things and it helps you. I know when I've gone to church I felt much better and was helped tremendously but I can't see life consisting just in this.

Pastor: You feel then that singing, praying, and church attendance is all there is to the Christian life and this takes away all of your fun?

Mrs. R: Yes.

Mrs. R is in open rebellion against her mother's most cherished way of life. "Worldliness" is to her an assertion of independence, of acceptance by the adult group to which she belongs. Since her mother defined religion as the avoidance of drinking, card-playing, and smoking, Mrs. R uses these same taboos to explain her own lack of religious commitment. So long as the pastor talks of these things, she will stay where she is.

But if the pastor could inquire into the way that Mrs. R feels about religion for herself, the interview might change. If she could see that there is a difference between rebellion against her mother and rebellion against God, there would be some opportunity for her to make a decision on her own. She seems to drift with the crowd like an adolescent who wishes approval above all else. Could Mrs. R ever understand that her unwillingness to be an adult person in her own right is the true cause of her separation from God?

There are other persons who know quite well why they are alienated from God. The conspicuous failures of their lives loom up before them. In the midst of their dilemmas, they neither trust God nor obey him. This is their sin. In despair and loneliness they feel themselves far from the Saviour whom they need.

For example, Mr. H, a thirty-year-old tenant farmer, had been visited several times by a Baptist pastor. On each visit Mr. H would say that he didn't have the "feeling" he needed for salvation. During the third visit, the pastor said:

PASTOR: Well, have you thought any more about what we talked about when I was here last?

MR. H: Yes, I think about it quite often.

PASTOR: What about you, Mrs. H? Has coming to church helped you with your feeling?

MRS. H: No, but I have been thinking about it a lot lately.

PASTOR: I believe last time we talked you both said that there was nothing that actually kept you from becoming Christians. Is that still true?

MR. H: Yes, I guess its just a matter of doing it.

PASTOR: Just a matter of *making* the decision?

MR. H: Yes (*as he drops his head*).

PASTOR: I sure would like to see you make this decision. You could do this tonight. (*There is a very long pause.*)

MR. H (*looking up*): Can a man have two living wives?

PASTOR: There are many who do. What do you mean?

MR. H: I have been divorced, and my wife is still living.

PASTOR: Do you feel that this stands in your way of becoming a Christian?

MR. H: Well—I don't know. I feel like I have sinned, because I don't believe in divorce.

PASTOR: We must look at the biblical idea here. We recognize that the ideal of God in marriage does not hold to divorce. He does not intend for men to divorce. But we must also see the other side and see that if divorce is a sin, God also forgives this sin. Do you feel that God would forgive you?

MR. H: —Yes—I guess so.

PASTOR: You must remember that God is willing to forgive you and you start your life with him anew. You and your wife can start your life over with one another and with Christ. (*turning to wife*) You have been divorced?

MRS. H: Yes.

PASTOR: This is what Jesus meant by being "born again" and what Paul means by becoming a "new creature."

MRS. H: Well, the divorce was not his fault. This was his first marriage, but his wife's second. I was my first husband's fourth wife. But I was young and didn't know what I was doing.

PASTOR: Divorce itself is against God's will. In fact, your former marriages may have been against God's will . . . but the thing is that even though a mistake has been made, once we recognize it and ask God to forgive, he will. Do you believe he will?

MR. H: Yes,—but I don't believe in divorce and I just can't forgive myself.

PASTOR: Why not?

MR. H: Well, you see, I was never really married. That is, in God's sight. I was married legally (*pause*). You see I had what is called a "common law" marriage. In Ohio if you live with a woman six months you are legally married and, therefore, have to get a divorce. I lived with her for four years and had one child.

PASTOR: So because you made this mistake you cannot forgive yourself and hate yourself for it?

MR. H: I certainly do. I have never been able to forgive myself.

PASTOR: This is one of the things about sin. We are always going to bear the scars and consequences for it, no matter if we have been forgiven. I would not try to tell you that you can forget this thing, because it is a part of you, especially since you have this child, whom you should continue to love.

MR. H: Oh, I certainly do.

PASTOR: Because you feel that this is sin, you are going to have to live with it. But I would say that when you have God's forgiveness, that of your family (*turns to wife and she nods her head*), and that of your friends, even though you will remember this thing, you can also remember—"I have been forgiven." Although you will never completely forget it, it will begin to fade. Christ offers a new life . . . let him take care of the past as well as the present and the future. Do you think you could believe in him that much? He doesn't ask us to come to him spotless. Remember the story of the adulterous woman . . . whom Jesus forgave and said to those around her, "Let him that is without sin cast the first stone." Do you think you could believe this?

MR. H: I don't know. I think about it all the time.

PASTOR: Remember, we have a great God . . . one that is not like a lot of people. He doesn't hold grudges, but is willing to forgive. And he will forgive you. (MR. H *with head down begins to shake his head.*)

Some of the pastor's assurances are theoretically correct, but Mr. H cannot hear them. The integrity of his self-image is destroyed. To him, divorce is the admission of ultimate failure in marriage. He now stands dejected, condemned by his own standards.

What if the pastor had turned from his sermonettes to ask: "What have you been taught about failure?" or "How have you experienced forgiveness in the past?" These questions would move behind the legal problem of divorce into a deeper level of interpersonal relations: the experience of past forgiveness or hardness of heart, the present acceptance of responsibility for hurt to others, a willingness to admit that no further action will help what is past, an admission of a shattered ego and of powerlessness to forgive self, a desire to be remade by God as a forgiven man.

There are still other persons whose separation from God cannot be attributed to gross personal failure. Theirs is more of a longing for a God who will love them, a community that will care for them. Like a middle-aged lady, Mrs. L, they want to know that they no longer carry their burdens alone. Mrs. L was recovering from an eye operation when a pastor visited her in the hospital.

MRS. L: I'm doing fine, considering everything I guess.

PASTOR: That's a fine attitude. It's not always easy to feel that way.

MRS. L: I guess it isn't, but that's the way I feel about it.

PASTOR: What do you think has helped you to come to feel this way?

MRS. L: Well, I just think about what could have happened to me.

I'm lucky to have come out of this as good as I did. A person could lose both of anything—like a limb, or something. Both of my eyes could have been injured. As it happened, only one of them was injured. I'm thankful for that.

PASTOR: In comparison to the many things that could have happened to you, you feel that you are fortunate to have come out as well as you did?

MRS. L: That's right.

PASTOR: Do you have a family of your own?

MRS. L: Yes, I have three children. I miss them very much. That's one reason I would like to get well so that I could be with them. But, I am not worried about them, or anything like that. My mother is taking care of them. I can just concentrate on getting well.

PASTOR: It is good to know that you have a dependable person who can take care of them until you are better. I am sure that they will miss you, too. What about your husband, has he been in to see you and tell you the news about the childen?

MRS. L: My husband is in the penitentiary.

PASTOR: Oh, I see (*pause*). That probably means you have had to take on some added responsibilities yourself then.

MRS. L: I hope this won't sound disrespectful—you being a pastor and everything—but actually things are much better for me now that he's gone. Some of my friends think it's awful for me to say that. But they don't know the trouble and misery that goes on inside the house when the shades are down. They don't know how he treated me and the family.

PASTOR: Now that he's gone, you think that you are better off?

MRS. L: That's right. Now I can do some things with my children that I couldn't do before. I can take them places and buy them things that I couldn't before.

PASTOR: I'm sure you are looking forward to doing some of these things with your children.

MRS. L: Yes, I am.

PASTOR: Tell me, is this your home town?

MRS. L: No, I was brought up in New Jersey. Later, I moved to Georgia. When I got married, we came here.

PASTOR: I see. I didn't know. I don't believe you are a member of our church.

MRS. L: No, I'm not a member of any church.

PASTOR: Have you ever thought about becoming a Christian?

MRS. L: Yes, I have. I feel that it is something that is important, and that it is something everyone should do. I certainly intend to do it.

PASTOR: Were you brought up in a church in New Jersey?

MRS. L: Yes, I was brought up in the Baptist church. My mother and
father belong to the church.

PASTOR: Why do you think you never did become a Christian?

MRS. L: I don't know. There have been times when I felt like something held me back. It was like something inside holding me back.

PASTOR: What did you think it was that was holding you back?

MRS. L: I don't exactly know. I can't exactly describe it. But, I do
feel that I will become a Christian some day.

PASTOR: This thing that you say was holding you back. It reminds me
of what we as Christians call original sin. It is rebelling against God
and thinking that we can get along without God in our lives. Do
you think this could have been your experience?

MRS. L: I don't know. I never had thought of it that way. It could
be. Perhaps I was holding back because I didn't think I needed
God.

Mrs. L feels that she is lost in her worry over children, trouble
with her husband, concern for her eye, and desire to be working
again. She is awakened to her need for strength beyond herself.
How will she receive it? The answer to this question takes us to
another central aspect of conversion, the acceptance of Christ.

Acceptance of Christ

How are we to be delivered from loneliness, meaninglessness,
pride, sensuality? The Christian answer to separation from God
is the mediation of Christ Jesus. Through him we have access to
a Heavenly Father. The life, death, and resurrection of his Son
have broken down the wall of hostility which separates God from
his creatures (Eph. 2). Our acceptance of Christ's mediation
brings salvation.

Mrs. L had said: "I didn't think I needed God"; the pastor
asked: "Has anyone ever talked to you before about becoming a
Christian?"

MRS. L: Yes, they have. But I never did quite see it the way you
put it.

PASTOR: The reason I asked was that I noticed in your answers that
you seem to already know about many of the things I'm saying.

MRS. L: Yes, I was brought up in Sunday school and church.

PASTOR: Then, you probably already know that you can become a

Christian right now. If you are willing to commit your life to Christ as your Lord, then he will become your Saviour. You can surrender your life to Christ right now. Of course, this means that you are surrendering the life now that you will live out for him each day. If you will make this surrender of your life to him, then he will become your Saviour. How does this sound to you? Does it speak to your life?

MRS. L: Yes, it does. I have heard these same things before, but I never had quite seen them like I do now.

PASTOR: Why do you think you see them differently now?

MRS. L: I don't know. All day today I have felt differently. Now, you have come and talked to me about becoming a Christian. And, it just seems that this is what I want to do.

PASTOR: Then, this is what you want to do right now?

MRS. L: Yes, it is.

For Mrs. L, acceptance of Christ included a willingness to admit her own frailty and trust in an eternal strength, Jesus Christ. In subsequent interviews, the implications of this trust were developed as she grew in the understanding of Christian commitment.

The individual interpretations of the initial acceptance of Christ are innumerable. Examples of this were found in the study of a "First Church" revival in 1961. Forty-one converts of that meeting in a Baptist church were interviewed.[24] Some of their interpretations of the "decision for Christ" were as follows:

(1) This was a confession of faith, a commitment, a life for Jesus.

(2) The decision was a time of forgiveness: "It was necessary for me to confess my sins to God and to the congregation; I felt like I was asking God to forgive me." Another convert said: "I went to the front of the church during the invitation and felt clean." It was a new chance to do right.

(3) Acceptance of Christ brought benefits—the assurance of heaven, assurance that life was no longer wasted.

(4) Acceptance of Christ implied change for the better in a convert's life or a public statement that he wanted to change.

(5) Acceptance of Christ resolved doubt. A teen-ager stated that

[24] I am grateful to Liston Mills, who organized the data as part of his Th.D. dissertation, and to the members of my graduate seminar: Leon Morris, Bill Mathis, Nathan Brooks, George Bennett, Ray Cooley, Ezra Luesson, Bob Whitten.

he had been arguing about the existence of God since he was eleven
years old. Now he knew God personally.

(6) Acceptance of Christ meant a decision of ultimate meaning,
one that is lifelong, in which God is the center.

(7) The decision for Christ was defined as a feeling: "I felt
happy," "I felt right," "felt clean."

Other types of answers stressed the "bigness" of the decision
or its difficulty, its spontaneity or reflectiveness, and its au-
tonomy: "This was *my* decision," "Mom didn't tell me what to
do, like other times."

These are the converts' thoughts in response to an interviewer's questions. Those to whom these persons are well
known may see more or less evidence of their decision. Ulti-
mately, of course, the mysterious power of God's salvation is
beyond description. But these replies may help pastors to understand how some people feel that Christ has saved them.

The Symbol of Commitment

The public seal of commitment by the convert and acceptance
by the church is baptism. The New Testament explanation of
baptism includes many elements of conversion and evangelism.
First, a profession of faith precedes baptism. The book of Acts
records that the Ethiopian eunuch, Cornelius, and the Philippian jailer were immersed after their confessions of Christ as
Saviour (Acts 8:34–38; 10:22–48; 16:29–34). This requirement distinguished Christian baptism and evangelism from
Jewish circumcision, a rite required of all male children. One
entered the Christian faith not by birth, but by belief.

Second, baptism is a symbol of the confession, belief, and
commitment which brings salvation (Rom. 10:9). The lowering
and raising of a person in water is a dramatic illustration of the
death of an old life and the beginning of a new life in Christ
(Rom. 6:1–11).

Baptism is not the saving act; the saving act took place in the
death and resurrection of Christ and the believer's acceptance of
that way of life for himself. For this reason the early church was
careful to teach candidates about Christ's life and to examine

their own lives before baptism. Without these—confession, belief, and commitment—baptism becomes a prefunctory rite for those who walk down a church aisle or a magical means of grace for the children of pious parents.

The concrete events of Christ's sacrifice and the believer's consecration provide the setting in which the drama of baptism is performed. These are essential because baptism is a sign of a change in life (1 Peter 3:21). He who is buried with Christ in baptism symbolizes his death to the elemental spirits of the world. He has been raised to a new life in Christ (Col. 2:8 to 3:4).

Third, baptism is a declaration of the convert's union with Christ and with his church. This is a voluntary union on the part of the believer, by which he becomes a part of the community gathered out of the world for God. The New Testament church demonstrated its freedom from the world by accepting candidates without distinction of race or class. Baptism is to be the visible bond between all believers (1 Cor. 12:13; Gal. 3:28; Col. 3:11). Some of the most damning evidence of worldliness in the church today is the refusal of some churches to receive persons of another race for baptism. If baptism is to regain its original significance, there must be renewed sacrifice and surrender both by the church and the candidate.

Fourth, baptism is the sign of new selfhood to the convert and a confirmation of his calling both by God and the church. For the older child or adolescent, it is an open declaration of allegiance to God, even above his own family. For the adult, it is the acceptance of responsibility for Christian attitudes—at home, at work, and in the community. Baptism is the church's confirmation of this call to be a new self in Christ. It is also an acceptance of open dedication to one way of life. This was boldly symbolized by Christ when he underwent baptism by John. In this public act he affirmed his acceptance of his Father's will (Matt. 3:13–17). For the adult, baptism is like a wedding ceremony. It is a public sign of responsibility for an intimate relationship. This is declared by the convert and confirmed by the church. As the Holy Spirit descended openly upon Christ at his baptism, so the immersion of his disciples is a symbol of the work which the Spirit of God has already begun in their lives.[25]

The Household of Faith

When a baptized believer becomes a part of the gathered community of Christ—the church—his separation from God and man is ended. As the body of Christ, the church is a partnership where people share a common devotion to Christ and have opportunity to connect inward life with outward conduct through the transforming power of the Spirit.[26]

The entrance of a convert into this partnership is sometimes blocked by the unworthy behavior of church members, interpersonal conflicts, differences in social attitudes, or the pastor's overemphasis upon the church organization.

To take the last of these first, there are some pastors who seem to be more concerned with the church than with the person. For example:

PASTOR A: Mr. S, we are still looking for you and Mrs. S to come with your children to church.

MR. S: Well, we just haven't gotten around to coming yet. We will try to do that some day.

PASTOR A: We were glad to have the children there and want you to decide to come with them. Are you going to any other church yet?

MR. S: No.

The interview continued and ended as a battle over church attendance.

Even when the pastor shows personal concern, evangelism may be blocked by interpersonal conflicts or the negative witness of a church member. In one instance, Mr. H said to a minister:

[25] See Karl Barth, *The Teaching of the Church Regarding Baptism, op cit.;* A. Gilmore (ed.), *Christian Baptism* (Philadelphia: Judson Press, 1959); R. E. O. White, *The Biblical Doctrine of Initiation* (Grand Rapids: William B. Eerdmans Publishing Co., 1960); H. H. Rowley, "The Christian Sacraments," *The Unity of the Bible* (Philadelphia: The Westminster Press, 1955); T. C. Smith, "Baptism," in *Encyclopedia of Southern Baptists,* ed. Norman W. Cox (Nashville: Broadman Press, 1958).

[26] See L. S. Thornton, *The Common Life in the Body of Christ* (Napierville, Ill.: Alec R. Allenson, Inc., 1950).

MR. H: I've thought a lot about the church and joining, but then I want to really be a Christian, I mean all the way.

PASTOR: Mr. H, from God we get that assurance. What seems to bother you about being a Christian?

MR. H: I'm hot-headed and every time I look at Brother S, I get real mad and that's not the Christian way. (*Brother S is a member of our church, who hurt very deeply H's brother-in-law and now the whole family has little to do with church.*)

PASTOR: Mr. H, the Christian life is a growth and I feel that you can grow out of this. Does your anger toward him stem from what happened to A?

MR. H: It sure does; I look at Mr. S and get mad. I hear him talk so pious and yet he's not. What if I were a Christian like that?

PASTOR: Mr. H, it is good you recognize this. It can be a steering point for you, can't it?

MR. H: I just don't know; I want to be sure.

PASTOR: I want you to be sure. Would you like to pray about this matter?

MR. H: Yes, that will be the only answer. (*After a prayer he said he would be at the services that night.*)

Pastor's evaluation: We concluded on a high note but Mr. H has neither joined the church nor made a profession of faith. I feel that I failed in this interview to bring out the true meaning of an experience.

Another obstacle is the social class of a particular church. Some churches minister to more than one stratum of society, but others are identified with "society," "workmen," "town," "mill," or "country." Each of these labels attracts some and repels others.

Social class is revealed in the architecture of the church, greeting and appearance of the ushers, form of service, manner of the minister, dress and attitudes of the congregation. One young lady who was in a strange city recognized this problem. She discussed it with a minister who was seeking to win her to membership in his church:

MISS E: I do enjoy your church.

PASTOR: Do you feel that it meets your needs—in a spiritual way?

MISS E: It's hard to say. Some things are different from where I grew up. Some things I understand and some I don't.

PASTOR: Did your church back home help in ways that we are not able to?

MISS E: In a way, I guess. It seems like back there I just couldn't help going forward. They had an altar where they prayed over people, and they all prayed out loud and at the same time. . . . But at your church it's different. Your people don't talk to me at all, either before or after the service.

Miss E feels like a displaced person. The coolness of the people confirms her suspicions of their restrained form of worship.

Probably the most formidable barrier to seekers is raised by the past conduct of church members. Those who represent themselves as Christians do not bear witness to a redeemed and holy life. The repelling influence of such persons was made clear to one pastor who had tried in vain to reach a prospect for his church by phone and letter. Finally, when he heard that the man in whom he was interested had just received a promotion, he made another phone call:

PASTOR: Mr. V, I have just received the good news of your new position. Your friend, Mr. R, told me that you had waited a long time for it. He seemed very happy for you.

MR. V: Yeah, thanks, Preacher.

PASTOR: As you know, I have looked forward to visiting you for some time. Would a time like this be good for a visit?

MR. V: I don't think so. Things look one way to me and another way to you. When I get interested in the church I expect to live like I'm supposed to. I don't now, and I'm not proud of it—but some of your members act one way Saturday night and another Sunday morning.

PASTOR: You've had some personal experience with this?

MR. V: You're ——— right I have! I'm a musician, and I used to play at the club that some of your biggest members go to. Ha! You should have seen them last New Year's Eve, gettin' drunk and slobbering over other men's wives. Don't tell me that they got religion.

PASTOR: I'm not. But maybe if we—

MR. V: Naw, I got a job now where I don't have to see those guys any more. I want to keep it that way (pause). Thanks anyway, Preacher.

PASTOR: O.K. If things change, or you need me, I'm here.
MR. V: I know. I'll see you sometime.

Opportunities for direct pastoral contact are closed in this case. If the pastor can find a devout layman who is respected by Mr. V, then the barrier may be crossed. It will not be easy. Mr. V has weighed "Christian" conduct against Christian teaching and found the church wanting.

A pastoral approach to these problems requires two emphases: the church is the family of God within which his people face their difficulties; barriers to church fellowship are as serious as a family split. Disregard of the latter emphasis may lead to coercion:

MR. B: Well, I just can't join the church while *that* family runs things. . . .
PASTOR: Now, Mr. B, you're big enough to overlook all that, I'm sure.
MR. B: Would you? Listen, Preacher. J said some things about my daughter that I wouldn't repeat about anybody. Her name was smeared all over town. But J and his wife walk about your church like they own everything.
PASTOR: But you must think about *God's* requirement. Compare your life to Christ. Are you so good?
MR. B: No. I don't pretend to be like *some* people.
PASTOR: Well then, you know your need of Christ. Will you look over these little things and see the great needs. We try to meet them in the church.
MR. B: Yeah. Well, maybe, some day.

The pastor counts Mr. B's resentment as a "little thing." He ignores the pointed question: "What would *you* do if someone spread scandal about your daughter?"

Our answers to such questions will reveal our concept of the church. If it is a fellowship of believers, then all who belong to it must face interpersonal questions. How can we love God and hate our brother (1 John 4:20)? What will the unbelievers think if we do not understand one another (1 John 3:19–25)? Will not the church be consumed by those who bite and devour one another (Gal. 5:13–15)? How can we worship God when we are not reconciled to each other (Matt. 5:23–24)? The rush of some pastors to ignore such questions is one reason for the decline of their church fellowship.

The church is a new family in God. For some it will be an affirmation of relationships already established in a godly home. For others it will be a new home, a better dwelling place. This last condition was found in one pastor's interview with a young lady who despised her own home and companions. She contrasted this with the wholesome life of new friends she had made in the church and the boardinghouse. Finally she said: "Oh, if I could just get what it takes and really be a Christian, I would be happy."

PASTOR: You have been attending our Sunday school and you have a wonderful teacher. (*Her teacher had taken a great deal of interest in her.*) Also, you have been attending our worship services off and on for over a year. You have heard again and again the story of the gospel and what you have to do to become a Christian. You want to be loved and nobody in all this world loves you any more than does our Heavenly Father. He loved you so much that he gave his Son, Jesus Christ, that if you will yield yourself to him and commit your life into his hands, he will grip your entire life and give you inner peace and satisfaction. He will help you to make adjustments that you can never make without his aid.

MISS: Somehow I feel that everything is going to work out for me. Oh, I do hope so. I want to love and be loved by everyone.

PASTOR: You have come seeking, and I know that. In Christ you will find God's love manifested to you and his love in your heart will make you love others. We are going to have prayer and I want you to go home and think seriously about this matter of trusting Christ as your Saviour. You will have opportunity to make this decision public at the close of our services tomorrow. Will you do that?

MISS: Yes, Sir. Thank you for taking time to talk with me. I feel lots better. Your wife has been a blessing to me. She has led me to see that I should get spiritual help from spiritual people.

PASTOR: We will help you any way we can. I appreciate your interest and congratulate you for pouring out your heart. A good confession can do great things for us. See you in church tomorrow.

In the church this young woman found new brothers and sisters. The godly matron of her boardinghouse was a mother-in-

God to her. The pastor and his wife were models of a Christian couple. As the pastor and the congregation continue to love and cherish her, she will find a better family in this household of faith.

The Committed Life

Conversion is a continual commitment of life to Christ. Helping new Christians to stand fast in this commitment is an essential feature of the pastor's ministry. We are to be as the apostle Paul who returned to new congregations, "strengthening the souls of the disciples, exhorting them to continue in the faith" (Acts 14:21). He urged the Colossian church to "continue in the faith, stable and steadfast, not shifting from the hope of the gospel which you heard" (Col. 1:23). Commitment to Christ is established and nourished through personal relationships. It is the evangelist's responsibility to root the gospel in the daily world of the convert. The redemptive work of God must be enmeshed with the attitudes, hopes, fears, family, and work of the individual.

These relationships were a vital part of commitment in the "First Church" study described earlier in this chapter. When a husband and wife came together during the revival and asked for church membership, they tended to become regular or very active members of the congregation. The same was true when a parent and child came together. Also, when children were influenced by their parents over a period of time to join the church, the children tended to become faithful members. But when children were quickly asked to join by the evangelist or pastor and had no parental support, they soon became inactive. Without rootage in good relationships, the tender tree of new life cannot bear fruit.

These channels of commitment are neglected by some pastors who are preoccupied with verbal prescriptions for faith. They substitute mechanical recitation of doctrine for the faithful and loving care that is the true ground for evangelism. If unsaved persons will only *say* the right words, these pastors are satisfied. They may use the "repeat-after-me" device. The unfeeling spirit of this approach may be seen in the call of Rev. E upon Dr. H:

REV. E: You wanted to talk with me about joining the church?

DR. H: Ah, well, yes, I guess so. You see, I am recovering from a liver infection. My colleagues tell me it is chronic and that I will always have some trouble from it. It's got me to thinking about all the patients I have treated who have chronic diseases. I think I'll be more patient with them. I didn't listen too much to them, and now I need someone to help me.

REV. E: Well, that's too bad, Doctor. Now tell me, are you a Christian?

DR. H: Ah, I guess so.

REV. E: Oh, a Christian should *know* his salvation. Have you ever made a public profession of faith?

DR. H: No.

REV. E: Do you believe Christ saves you from sin?

DR. H: Ah, well, I believe in God, and I know that I should trust him. . . .

REV. E: But will you trust in Christ to save you now?

DR. H: I would like to. I guess I need something. These blue moods have just about gotten me down.

REV. E: Jesus will take care of that. Just trust him. Will you kneel down with me now? (*Both kneel.*) Now, Doctor, I want you to pray after I do. "Lord, look down now and save this good doctor. Heal him, Lord, and we'll give you the victory. Amen." Now you pray, Doctor.

DR. H: God, help me to do better. . . .

REV. E: Now say after me, "Jesus I accept you as my Saviour. . . ."

DR. H: Jesus, I accept you as my Saviour. . . .

REV. E: "Forgive me for my sins. . . ."

DR. H: Forgive me for my sins. . . .

REV. E (*rising*): Now! Doctor, you are a saved man! I brought with me some literature on my church. You read this and you'll know what the church is all about. Tells all about our committees, budget, and organization. Can we look for you in church soon?

DR. H: I'd like to come when I can.

REV. E: Good! Then I'll be going, and God bless you in your decision for Christ.

DR. H (*shakes hand of* REV. E): Thank you for coming. I am at my wit's end. I need to talk to someone.

REV. E: Yes, yes, of course (*backs out front door*).[27]

---

[27] For the skeptical reader, I was an eyewitness to this entire incredible performance.

Has Dr. H seen the relation of his suffering and depression to the Christian faith? Has a man of God come to share these with him? No. Rev. E has come to "win him to Christ," by which he means getting Dr. H to repeat a set of verbal propositions. This ritual intonation is Rev. E's equivalent for commitment of life to Christ. Rev. E left the home convinced that he had "won a soul for the Lord." He did not have much time to think about it, however, since he had ten more calls to make before the afternoon was over.

As the seed of the gospel is planted, so will the life grow. Those who are forced-fed on slogans may die of spiritual malnourishment. Those who are taught to find Christ in their personal relationships are on the way to a more abundant life.

The Unity of Personality

The problems of life commitment often have been avoided by splitting an individual into "body" and "soul." For example, Rev. E had no time for a discussion of Dr. H's depression, physical illness, or loneliness. These would be aspects of the "body." Rev. E. was "going after the man's soul." This is poor theology, as well as poor pastoral care.

Some modern theologians have re-emphasized New Testament teachings on the unity of personality.[28] Paul and other writers of the first century stressed the wholeness of man. Holiness is wholeness, the restoration of a divided self torn by the pleasures of the senses (Rom. 1) or a break between the love for God and love for men (1 John). The evangelistic challenge of the Bible is not to save a disembodied "soul" but to accept the total commitment of Christ's command: "You shall love the Lord your God with all your heart, and with all your soul, and with all your mind . . . [and] your neighbor as yourself" (Matt. 22:37–39).

Converts who accept this challenge are often in need of pastoral care. One of these was Mr. Fry, who at the age of fifty

[28] D. R. G. Owens, *Body and Soul* (Philadelphia: The Westminster Press, 1956); Aubrey Johnson, *Vitality of the Individual in the Thought of Ancient Israel* (Cardiff: University of Wales Press, 1949); J. A. T. Robinson, *The Body: a Study in Pauline Theology* (Chicago: H. Regnery, 1952).

became a Christian after twenty years of steady drinking. Within a year after his conversion, Mr. Fry was a sober member of the church and community. But every improvement in his living increased the gap between himself and the wife who had lived with his drunkenness for twenty years. She was now seen to be indifferent to even the simplest household duties. Mr. Fry wanted a clean house now, so he had to clean it. He wanted the children to attend church, so he had to dress all four of them each Sunday morning while his wife slept. He now held a steady job, but she squandered all he gave her on trifles. What was he to do?

The pastor who reported this case said that he might have promised Mr. Fry a bright future if he would "have faith." But the pastor was unwilling to deceive this struggling Christian. Therefore, he told Mr. Fry that the way was harder now than before because his new standards brought his old way of life into glaring contrast. Because of years of abuse, Mr. Fry could not expect his wife to change automatically into a charming housekeeper. Mr. Fry might have to do more than his share around the home.

At the same time, the pastor promised to talk with Mrs. Fry about her attitudes toward Mr. Fry and the implications of his change for her home. When he did this, the pastor found Mrs. Fry to be so apathetic that he had to teach her step by step the relationship of Christian standards to cleanliness, thrift, orderliness, and cheerfulness. The task is by no means complete, but Mr. Fry knows that the pastor shares his commitment to the salvation of an entire family. This new Christian was not abandoned as a saved "soul" without a body of personal relations.

6

The Evangelism of Children

The evangelism of children requires patience of the pastor and responsibility in the child. Pastoral patience includes loving care and righteous discipline. These are characteristics of "pastoral" evangelism.[1] The patient exercise of mercy and discipline by the pastor must be correlated with the child's responsible and decisive actions and attitudes.

The balance of patience and responsibility will vary from one denomination to another and also within a denomination. Liturgical communions have tended to institutionalize patience and nonliturgical groups have emphasized responsibility.

Patience has been formalized by some denominations as infant baptism, catechetical classes, and confirmation. Pastor, parent, and child move by these stages toward full church membership for the child. Each communion solves the problem of patience and responsibility in a different way. Among Episcopalians, the church is the repository of both patience and responsibility for the child. Through the sacrament of baptism, the infant is provided with saving grace. Responsibility for his salvation is taken by the church. The full action of God in baptism must be completed by the spiritual care which parents, godparents, and priest provide for the child.[2] Catechetical classes prepare the child for confirmation by the bishop as a responsible church member.

When the church takes responsibility and patience to itself, the danger is that most of the responsibility may stay with the

[1] See *supra*, pp. 7–8.
[2] Reuel Howe, *Man's Need and God's Action* (Greenwich, Conn.: The Seabury Press, 1953) is a guide for parents and godparents.

83

church and little will be transferred to the child. Pastor Jacob Andreasen described this problem in *Lutherans and Conversion*. Out of 580 Lutheran respondents who were baptized as infants, only 27 per cent claimed on a questionnaire that they had remained in baptismal grace. The majority, 63 per cent, wrote that they fell away from God and were converted in adolescence or adulthood.[3] Their sense of spiritual responsibility remained dormant or infantile.

Presbyterians and Methodists use institutionalization of patience to transfer responsibility from church to child. There is less emphasis upon the saving grace of a sacrament than among Episcopalians and Lutherans. Instead, more stress is laid upon family and church relationships. Infant baptism is a ceremony in which parents and pastor pledge themselves to surround the child with Christian fellowship and teaching. About the age of nine to twelve, children enter a class of instruction which will prepare them for full membership in the church. Under the influence of Horace Bushnell, Presbyterians have tended to interpret this as an uninterrupted process in which the child always knows himself to be a Christian. Methodists "consider the pastor's class the basic evangelistic thrust" for the children of the church.[4]

One of the major problems in the transfer of responsibility is that salvation will come through education rather than through personal decision. The gradual, evolutionary presuppositions of early twentieth-century education have replaced nineteenth-century expectations of personal commitment which might be wrought out in a crisis decision. The former dean of Louisville Presbyterian Seminary, Lewis J. Sherrill, in an address on "The Evangelism of Children," offered this interpretation:

The modern religious education movement is in danger of unintentionally identifying itself with the early medieval church in its conception of child evangelism. The medieval church, seeking to make

[3] Jacob Andreasen, *Lutherans and Conversion* (Minneapolis: T. S. Denison & Co., 1955), p. 114.
[4] Personal correspondence from Mary Alice Jones, General Board of Education, The Methodist Church, June 24, 1955.

a place for children, brought them in early and completely by means of sacraments, but lost the conception of personally confronting the church's children with Christ, and pressing them for their own committal to Him. In modern religious education, we have replaced the sacraments with education as the means of grace; we have brought children into the fellowship of the church early and completely by means of education; and we have tended to surrender any definable evangelism, thus leaving the way open either to ignore it or to turn it over to the revivalist. Thus we have virtually duplicated the medieval conception, but with a new terminology.[5]

A crisis decision is emphasized in denominations which practice responsibility with little patience. This seems to be most characteristic of those Baptist and Disciples of Christ groups which have thrived on the frontier tradition of evangelism. In complete contrast to liturgical communions, modern Southern Baptists place much responsibility upon the child and little or none upon the church. *His* decision carries so much finality that there are few efforts to care for his development by the pastor. Pastoral patience is seen neither in the preparation of the child for church membership nor in the growth that should follow conversion.

From a pastoral point of view, the present problem of all denominations is a balance of patience and responsibility in child evangelism. The institutionalization of patience by some communions has minimized the expectation of a definitive, autonomous commitment by the young communicant. The exaltation of private religious experience by other denominations has led to a neglect of patient nurture for new converts. One church feeds the child without awakening him, while another church awakens the child and does not feed him.

The Ripening of Spiritual Responsibility

The time of spiritual awakening has traditionally been discussed as "the age of accountability." A Jewish boy is "held

[5] Quoted in Gideon Yoder, *The Nurture and Evangelism of Children* (Scottdale, Pa.: Herald Press, 1959), p. 168. Professor E. G. Homrighausen of Princeton Seminary implies in *Choose Ye This Day* (Philadelphia: The Westminster Press, 1943) that something is lacking in a generation which has lost the ability to experience a spiritual crisis.

accountable for his own sins" at the age of puberty. The ceremony of *bar mizvah* proclaims the boy's power to comply responsibly with legal requirements. In churches that practice confirmation, the child is expected to be at the "age of discretion."

Professor T. G. Tappert of the American Theological Committee (Lutheran) considers early adolescence as the time when a child approaches the age of discretion.[6] Churches that expect a crisis experience believe that the child must see himself as a sinner when he reaches the "age of accountability." Salvation is interpreted to children as "forgiveness of sins" or "the time of beginning life for God." [7]

For the past sixty years there has been a steady drop in the chronological age at which churches will accept a child's accountability for sin. In 1899, Starbuck's study presented sixteen as the average age of conversion.[8] By 1929, Clark found that the average age was twelve.[9] In 1959, Jenkins' questionnaire to Baptist ministers in west Kentucky indicated that almost half of the persons baptized in their churches were between the ages of six and twelve.[10]

This steady move toward Primary-age conversion is not the result of theological pressure. There was pressure two hundred years ago, when Jonathan Edwards referred to children as "young snakes" and "children of the devil." [11] But by 1900, George Coe was describing normal child development as entirely within the kingdom of grace.[12] At the same time, the conservative theologian A. H. Strong wrote: "Certain and great as is the guilt of original sin, no human soul is eternally condemned solely for this sin of nature, but . . . all who have not

---

[6] Yoder, *op. cit.,* p. 75.

[7] Questionnaire distributed among pastors in St. Louis, Mo., and Paducah, Ky., and tabulated in Gerald Jenkins, "A Pastoral Care Study of the Religious Experiences of Children Six to Twelve Years" (Master's thesis, Southern Baptist Theological Seminary, Louisville, Ky., 1959), p. 31.

[8] *Op. cit.,* p. 33.

[9] *Op. cit.,* p. 63.

[10] Jenkins, *op. cit.,* pp. 29–30.

[11] John H. Gerstner, *Steps to Salvation: the Evangelistic Message of Jonathan Edwards* (Philadelphia: The Westminster Press, 1959), p. 78.

[12] George A. Coe, *Education in Religion and Morals* (Westwood, N. J.: Fleming H. Revell Co., 1904), p. 47.

consciously and wilfully transgressed are made partakers of Christ's salvation." [13]

An able Mennonite authority on child evangelism wrote in 1959: "The child is provided for in the atonement until he reaches the age of moral responsibility." [14] Since he is not spiritually endangered in childhood, his conversion should not be encouraged until he is morally and mentally mature.

From a study of the psychology of childhood and adolescence, Professor Yoder recommended early adolescence as the time when some children may be baptized as believers. They have reached the dawn of moral consciousness. Others should be encouraged to seek baptism in later adolescence, the time of mental maturity. Believers' baptism should not be recognized before adolescence, in Yoder's judgment, because the child has neither the moral awareness nor mental capacity to renounce his sinful nature. The confidence and trust of early childhood must not be confused with saving faith. Baptism is not a technique for holding youth in the church; it is the symbol of death to an old nature and new life in Christ.[15] How can an elementary child renounce himself when his personality is not fully formed and no agency of society (except churches) holds him morally responsible for his actions?

Psychological studies of childhood offer no support for responsible conversions at an early age. In his pioneer investigations of *The Moral Judgment of the Child,* Jean Piaget found that children of seven or nine years obey rules because older persons tell them to do so or because it is traditional. By the age of ten or twelve, the child is moral by mutual agreement. The kindergarten child operates under constraint; he respects his parents' commands as the law. By age twelve the child is motivated by co-operation, his sense of mutual respect for peers and parents is strong. Inwardly he feels the desire to treat others as himself. His rational judgment is developing to the place where he distributes justice according to individual needs.

[13] Strong, *op. cit.,* p. 357.
[14] Yoder, *op. cit.,* pp. 126–7.
[15] *Ibid.,* pp. 121–64.

These findings are substantiated by Robert Havighurst in *Human Development and Education*. In discussing values, he states: "It is not expected the child of nine will show up as having a well-formulated and flexible value system; but this gradual development progresses to near completion in adolescence." [16] About age twelve the child is just beginning to show the power of abstract thinking.[17] His major task is to change from an authoritarian to a rational conscience. That is, he must begin to accept moral principles as his own and interpret their application for himself. It is not enough for him to continue in unthinking obedience to the rules of parents.[18]

The studies of Piaget, Havighurst, and others [19] present childhood as the time of moral growth from parental obedience, through group relationships, to the dawning awareness of the Golden Rule in early adolescence. By age twelve or thirteen, a child is psychologically capable of understanding that he must do to others as he wishes them to do to him. If obedience to the Golden Rule were salvation, then the child would be ready for it. Since salvation is something other than this, pastoral patience is required.

Specifically, an older child or adolescent should be psychologically ready for three theological aspects of salvation: (1) the ability of theological abstraction, that is, to think of God as more than flesh and blood, to conceptualize sin as an attitude rather than a series of disobedient acts, to see salvation as an eternal event and not just a promise to do good now; [20] (2) the capability of independent action and judgment, rather than a submission to the parents' God and the definition of sin as disobedience to parents; (3) the awareness of an adult's re-

[16] Robert J. Havighurst, *Human Development and Education* (New York: Longmans Green & Co., 1953), p. 98.

[17] *Ibid.*, p. 90.

[18] *Ibid.*, p. 53. See also pp. 36, 53–54, 83, 98.

[19] Additional studies are presented in Yoder, *op. cit.*

[20] In personal correspondence (July 15, 1955) Dean Myron Hopper, College of the Bible, wrote: "Children are not theologians or philosophers. They do not deal with life in terms of generalizations and abstract ideas. They can "mouth" theological terms but these have little meaning for the child. If joining the church is to be on a theological basis, then children should not join. Early adolescence would be the earliest age."

sponsibilities as a church member and his contribution to the Christian community and to the world.

These requirements have been suggested by Professor William Hull of Southern Baptist Theological Seminary. From a study of the New Testament meaning of conversion and salvation, he has concluded that repentance and faith are possible only after an adolescent is aware of his rebellion against God.[21] The self-assertiveness of a child is not "sin"; it is an attempt to establish his identity toward parents. In adolescence, the problem is to achieve independence of the parents and dependence upon God.[22] Professor Hull has also concluded that conversion implies adult responsibility in the family and in the world. Children are not spoken of as "converted," but as "covenant" beings. The children of believing parents are holy because they are in the covenant, not because they are already converted (cf. 1 Cor. 7:14). Conversion requires a responsible, repentant attitude which is not possible until adolescence.

Churches that hold to believer's baptism are committed to repentance and faith as conditions of conversion. To fulfil the theological requirements of conversion, pastors must match love with judgment. Patiently they must use peer groups, parents, teachers, and their own personal contacts to prepare the child psychologically and spiritually for his own confession of faith. With discipline they must wait for the ripening of spiritual responsibility before the child is held capable of meeting theological requirements for baptism and church membership.

If these are the theological and psychological foundations of conversion, then why are so many Junior-age children received into churches that practice believers' baptism? The answer is to be found in the presuppositions of instant evangelism. First, this type of evangelism substitutes the affirmation of theological propositions for a warm, intimate knowledge of the inquirer's personality. A child, therefore, is accepted if he says yes to statements about the "plan of salvation." Second, instant

---

[21] Unpublished paper, "The Crisis in Child Evangelism."
[22] These last two sentences are derived from Lewis Sherrill's *Struggle of the Soul*.

evangelism is interested in a "soul" without reference to family or social relationships. In fact, evangelistic invitations may be made in Primary or Junior departments where only the adult teachers may protest. If parental resistance is anticipated, then, as one pastor said, "I baptize as many as I can get away with, without the parents' finding out."

Third, the impulsive nature of instant evangelism has little place for a probationary period or examination of the inquirer. The child's word is often taken as all that is required for an affirmative church vote. When there is parental pressure or the social expectation of early baptism, the pastor has no institutionalized procedure for delaying acceptance of the child. Fourth, immediate acceptance without training in the requirements of Christian faith and conduct leads to the almost complete lack of church discipline. The instant evangelist is pleased to hear a child say that he "loves Jesus." His inability to meet the exacting requirements of a mature Christian witness is disregarded.

The fifth assumption of instant evangelism leads to the most serious perversion of conversion. This is the uncritical acceptance of an inquirer's statement that he is anxious about his sins. When this is applied to children, the evangelist naturally finds that Primaries and Juniors do not know the Pauline meaning of sin as rebellion against God.[23] Since the plan of salvation requires a statement of sinfulness, the child is asked, "Well, did you ever disobey your parents?" When the child says yes, the evangelist moves on to the next proposition: "Do you believe that Jesus can save you?"

The evangelist has equated disobedience to parents with rebellion against God. The child is unthinkingly encouraged to form an idolatrous relationship, to believe that the words of mortal mothers and fathers are the eternal commands of the Creator.

---

[23] The relation of sin to evangelism is very important to Southern Baptists, who believe that "a child is accountable to God when he is able to understand, simply and basically, what sin is; that he himself is a sinner, that his sin is against God, and that he is under condemnation for it" (personal correspondence with Howard Colson, Sunday School Board, Southern Baptist Convention, July 6, 1955).

Is it any wonder that in adolescence, when young people natu-rally seek independence of their parents, many abandon the religion that was firmly riveted to parent-worship in the white heat of an evangelistic exhortation?

Instant evangelism has no plan for Christian growth. This is the sixth reason why it offers support to early baptism. Without a knowledge of childhood development, the instant evangelist as-sumes that the child is "ready" when he can say the words that adult converts say. Because the child is earnest and insistent, he is accepted. With no planned patience, the evangelist feels that an immediate decision is necessary. Delay means rejection when one thinks only of today.

In relation to children, instant evangelism fails the pastoral requirements of both patience and responsibility. The impatient evangelist has little care for the child before he professes faith and less time for his cultivation afterwards. The child's re-sponsibility is distorted by the evangelist's psychological igno-rance. Childish striving toward selfhood is equated with adult rebellion against God; the natural identity of children with their friends is accepted in place of a mature decision to be gathered out of the world into God's people. The impressionable willing-ness of a child to say yes before important adults is substituted for careful inquiry into a believer's motivation for new life in Christ.

While Norman Deaton, a youth evangelist, was writing his Th.M. thesis, he decided to look more closely at the conven-tional public invitations which he had been giving for Primary- and Junior-age children at the close of Vacation Bible school. He gave an invitation for the children to accept Christ as Saviour, and then talked privately with each child who came forward. When he asked each one why he came, he received multitudinous answers. Some of them went like this: "Because Johnnie came"; "I got tired of standing back there"; "I want to go to the bath-room." [24]

---

[24] "A Study of Postbaptismal Conversion" (Master's thesis, Southern Baptist Theological Seminary, Louisville, Kentucky, 1959), p. 90.

Postbaptismal Conversion

The fruit of impatient evangelism is an incomplete conversion. Half the children (age eight to twelve) in the "First Church" study mentioned in chapter 5 were inactive within a year after the revival in which they professed faith in Christ. What about the other half, those that retained some interest? In a few years some of them will be mature Christians who look with happiness upon their early decision. But others will confess that they "didn't know what was going on" when they joined the church. As their religious life deepens, they will repudiate their childhood decision and affirm that now, in the dawning of full maturity, they know the meaning of salvation. They may "rededicate" themselves or request "rebaptism."

In many instances the adolescent request for rebaptism is a symptom of former pastoral neglect. Mr. Deaton interviewed fifty adolescents (age sixteen to twenty) who had been baptized between the ages of eight and ten. Only one out of four had had more than ten minutes of conversation with their pastor when they made the original decision for Christ.[25] As adolescents, they looked back on those conversations, or the lack of them, and reported that their own solution was to hold their problems within. They had "things to talk about" at age eight or ten but the pastor had no time or interest to hear. Over half of the adolescents stated that they had no pastoral counsel of any kind when they joined the church as a child.[29]

Because of this neglect, they confessed to little understanding of the Christian faith, at that earlier age, and the ways by which they could become spiritually mature. Now, in later adolescence, these young people reported prolonged struggles with guilt and dissatisfaction with self. When these were resolved, the youths felt that they were really converted. Driven by typical adolescent idealism, they wished to "be honest," admit to the church that their first baptism was abortive, and request believer's baptism.

---

[25] *Ibid.*, p. 90. In a questionnaire to Baptist college freshmen, 27 per cent reported prebaptismal instruction. Jenkins, *op. cit.*, p. 46.

[26] Forty-five per cent in Jenkins' study received no instruction before or after baptism.

How may this unfortunate condition be avoided? In many ways this problem is similar to the remarriage of divorced persons. In both cases the person is asking that the church repeat itself through a second ceremony. It is good pastoral practice to investigate the reasons for rebaptism, just as pastors inquire into a person's background before remarriage. "How much have you grown up?" is an appropriate question in either case. Finally, the best answer in both cases is prevention—the cultivation of premarital and prebaptismal counsel.

The Practice of Pastoral Patience

To children, the pastor is the most significant person in their formal religious commitment. He is the one who offers them the opportunity to join the church, receives them, presents them to the congregation, and, in some cases, instructs them in the development of Christian faith. His patience is of primary importance.[27]

The need for pastoral patience has been demonstrated in the discussion of the "age of accountability" and postbaptismal conversion. How is a pastor to put this patience into practice? The ecclesiastical answer to this question would be a catechetical or disciples' class in one church and more informal counseling of individual children in another church.

Whatever the method, there are some interpersonal issues that must be faced. These are the child's relation to God, family, and the church; parental attitudes toward the child; the relation of the parents to the church; and the relation of the parents to each other. It takes some patience for a pastor to observe and deal with these complex interrelationships. But if he does so with grace, he will find that the child's motivation is clearer, his bond to the church is stronger, and the religious life of his

[27] In Jenkins' study, children baptized about the age of fourteen indicated that the pastor was the most significant person in their religious experience (35 per cent). Next in importance were mother (17.2 per cent), Sunday school teacher (9.7 per cent), and father (7.5 per cent). Children baptized at age twelve or under indicated that the preacher was most significant (32.3 per cent), then Sunday school teacher (20.6 per cent), mother (17.6 per cent), and father (8.9 per cent). *Op. cit.*, p. 45.

family is renewed. The family and the church are the ground to be cultivated by the pastor so that the seed of Christian faith may root and grow strongly in the child.

The illustrative material throughout the rest of this chapter is drawn from a pastor's conferences with individual children and a disciples' class for twelve Junior- and Intermediate-age boys and girls. The class was held eight weeks for half an hour during the opening assembly in Sunday school. Children and their parents were visited in their homes by the pastor during those eight weeks.

The Child's Motivation

A pastor's conversations with a child provide an opportunity for the child to demonstrate and learn the personal meaning of Christian faith. This involves the translating of doctrines into the daily life of home, church, school, and play.

When James Little [28] made a profession of faith at the close of a Sunday evening church service, the pastor invited him to come by his study after school the next day. As they talked Monday afternoon, James said that he had been thinking for several years that he was a Christian (he is now sixteen). He thought that baptism would not mean that he now became a new person, but that it would strengthen what he already believed and help him to be a witness to others.

"Now I can invite somebody to *my* church," he said. "It's good to be in a church with friends like Jack Burke. If somebody sees you going to church, it may influence him to go too."

The pastor asked James about the change of attitudes which characterized one who was proclaiming his Christian faith.

James replied: "Well, I get along well with everybody, but you like some people better than others. I like to see what the other fellow's point of view is and explain mine."

"That's a good point," said the pastor; "that's like Christian love, seeing the other's point of view and wishing the best for him."

[28] The name is fictitious, as are all others in the verbatim interviews and case studies.

"Yeah," said James, "like my father—I want the best for him. He's not a member of any church, and—well—now that I've decided, I wish he would too. He's good to me, and I think he'd like to join, but he drinks beer and doesn't want to give that up. He says he wants to do right when he joins."

"Well, James," said the pastor, "this is why I asked about attitudes instead of about actions. The major problem for a man is not giving up this or that, but admitting that he can't be righteous without God's help. Conversion means that his attitude toward himself and toward God is different. He now seeks God's guidance for what he does and thinks. He admits that he hasn't the strength to know or to do right by himself. . . ."

"Yeah, I see that," James interrupted. "Dad's a good guy. Of course I don't see him much now with school and all that. Ah, are you going to talk to him like you're talking to me?"

"Sure, but what about the way I'm talking to you?"

"Well," replied James, "I mean helping me to see that being a Christian is important stuff—I mean, that it's not just changing this or that, but like you say, seeing things different."

"That's good, James. You see what I'm saying, and I'll be glad to see your father." The interview ended with the pastor's prayer for the boy to understand his decision and thanksgiving for what he had already done.

In evaluating this conversation, one could first say that the pastor tried to maintain a balance between listening to the boy's needs and instructing him in the meaning of conversion. This is an appropriate combination of love and discipline. James told what church membership would mean to him and how much the pastor's questions and teaching meant to him. He did not say much about his own attitudes, but quickly turned to one of his chief concerns, the spiritual welfare of his father. In assuring the boy that he would talk to the father, the pastor missed an opportunity to ask how the boy saw things differently now that they had talked. He might also have asked how the father would be expected to see things. What does James hope for his father?

In subsequent interviews the pastor had opportunity to know both James and his father. The father confessed that he had been worried for some time about his own lack of religious commitment and thought that he "should do all he could to be a good example for his son." Several weeks later he was baptized with his son.

James talked enough for the pastor to know something of his motivation. But in conversations with other children, the pastor may find much reticence. For example, George Rudasall said nothing in the pastor's class and nothing to his family. The pastor suspected that his reserve may have been due to embarrassment concerning the steady drinking of his father, who had no contacts with the church community.

At the age of fourteen, George was beginning to feel keenly the difference between himself and children from more stable homes. The pastor never knew the boy well. George continued to be faithful in church attendance, although he did not join. Two years later he became interested in the Explorer Scouts and "opened up" to the leader of the troop. Through the Christian interest of this man, George began to express his pent-up embarrassments and eventually felt strong enough to test his new-found faith in himself by making a public profession of faith in Christ.

The children of very stable parents may also have little to say. In such an instance, the pastor must depend on the parents or friends for some interpretation of the child's motivation. Fred Miller was very passive. He gave intelligent answers to the pastor's questions about the Christian life, and Mrs. Miller reported afterward, "You have completely won him over." However, although Fred was consistent in his attendance both Sunday morning and Sunday evening, he did not make a public decision. Since he read a great deal, the pastor sought to prepare the soil for the future by recommending a number of books on his age level such as *The Church of Our Fathers* by Bainton and *The Dragon and the Book* by Price. History is Fred's special early adolescent craze.

Children can demonstrate their concern for Christ by both action and conversation. When this develops, it may be noticed by both the parents and the pastor. Their reaction may, as in the parable of Jesus, provide good soil or choke out the Word. The relationships of parent to child and of parent to parent may be stony ground. It is important, therefore, that the pastor be sensitive to the many factors in the family that influence a child's private and public allegiance to Christ and his church. Three of these will be considered in the rest of this chapter—communication of child with parents, parental attitudes toward the church, and parental ability to deal with conflicts that consciously involve the child.

Communication with Parents

A child's decision for Christ is stabilized and developed when there are excellent relationships with the parents in all areas of living. Such was the case with Margaret Gorman. Margaret's mother never allowed her active life in the church organizations to interfere with time reserved for her three children. This earned her some resentment from compulsive members of the church, but paid rich dividends in her family life. As Margaret said in talking privately to the pastor: "Mama may go off to a meeting when we go to school but she's always home before we are."

In the pastor's class Margaret asked whether Christians always had to pray publicly. When the pastor said that it depended upon many things, she broke in to say: "Well, Daddy won't ever pray in church, but he will read the Bible for us when we pray at home before we go to bed." This is the type of relationship that men preach about but seldom find in pastoral practice—even in the manse.

In contrast, John Seely was blocked on all levels of communication with his parents. Intellectually, they refused to see him join "because he's too young and doesn't know enough doctrine." This came from the father. The mother was more personal: "Until he stops playing mean tricks on other kids he's not worthy to be a member of the Baptist church." A perfectionistic, legalistic use of religion was characteristic of the parents' personalities. The boy's emotional response to his parents, even before he knew they rejected his independent move toward the church, was as follows:

PASTOR (in class): Now let's see how this business of loving neighbors works out in our own home. Are there times when it's hard to love somebody in our own family?

JOHN: Like who, for instance?

BOB THOMAS: I hit my little sister sometimes.

PASTOR: That's an example.

JOHN: Yeah, I do that, too.

PASTOR: Maybe it applies to parents, too.

JOHN: Ha! Lots of times I'd like to kill my father.

PASTOR: Lots of times?

JOHN: Sure, who wouldn't?

Actually, the pastor did not know the source of this rebellion or how much of it was healthy. It is known that whatever hostility existed was intensified by John's desire to become a church member. The father never mentioned it. John became sullen in church and sought to evade any responsibility in youth groups. Mrs. Seely has never mentioned her concern about John's conduct again. One hopeful sign is the relationship of John and a chum who is a church member. They sit together in church at all times. John's "buddy" is one positive link to the Christian fellowship.

A child's decision may block parental communication or it may be a lever to open new areas of understanding. Mr. and Mrs. Steadman were just as reserved about J. B. as the Seelys were about John. But they were willing to talk about things with the pastor and in the presence of the children. Superficially, their reasoning was the same as John's parents. Mrs. Steadman said: "I don't want him to do this until he knows what he's doing. Anyway, Preacher, I don't think he's quite good enough to join."

PASTOR: Good enough—how?

MRS. STEADMAN: Well, I guess I might as well be honest. We're not society folks. My boys are kept clean and neat, but they don't have much to wear. I feel like some folks look down on us. I don't want J. B. to be hurt. I want him to be a Christian, but I don't want him to be embarrassed by it, you understand?

PASTOR: You mean it's about clothes, and . . .

MRS. STEADMAN: Yes. And especially the fact that we have to go in a pickup truck. That really hurts my husband. He's a proud man.

PASTOR: Sure. I guess you just haven't noticed the pickup that Mr. Rowley drives because he parks on the side of the church.

MRS. STEADMAN: Why, is that so! Ed, you hear that?

MR. STEADMAN: I didn't know that. I—well, I guess that clears up something for me. I want my boys to be Christians. But I tell you, Preacher, it's not just society that keeps me out. It's things in me.

MRS. STEADMAN: Ed, you're not a wicked man. Brother Young, we both were raised where they preached a lot against all kinds of things. That's bothered me some, but I think it bothers Ed more. Now you preach. . . .

MR. STEADMAN: No, it's not just that.

PASTOR: You mean that there are things in your life that you know are wrong, no matter what anyone else says.

MR. STEADMAN: Yes, Sir. And I don't want my boys to see me join the church until I know I want to give up such things. J. B.'s a good boy. I'd be proud to see him join the church.

J. B. did make a public decision. The father publicly accepted Christ two years later. Mrs. Steadman, who has been a Baptist since childhood, began to come to church more often until her husband became sick and she was forced to stay at home with him. Although there was an initial barrier toward the church, it was not insuperable as with the Seelys. Open communication between child, parent, and pastor made the difference.

When the parental channels of love and grace are open and strong, a child like Margaret may be received into the church in late childhood or early adolescence. But this must be carefully investigated. The pastor may find that another "good Christian family," like the Seelys, provides no religious sustenance for the child's growth. Although chronologically older than Margaret, John at twelve had not received the kind of Christian support from his parents that enabled Margaret to make a responsible decision for Christ at eleven.

Parental Attitudes Toward the Church

The child's path toward salvation can be made clear or clouded by the parents' perception of organized religion. Abe Leslie had little to say to his father or mother about anything, but the father made an effort to talk about church membership with his son. Mr. Leslie even brought his son to the pastor and explained that Abe's terseness did not mean a lack of interest in becoming a Christian.

In one instance a father's positive attitude toward the church threw him into severe conflict when his son entered the pastor's class. The father, Mr. Cook, came to the pastor with much agitation and said: "I just don't know about Oscar's joining the church. He's just ten, you know. I didn't think you'd do a thing like that." After the pastor invited Mr. Cook into the study, the latter said: "I just don't go for these emotional decisions. I've seen enough of those in my time."

PASTOR: You've had some personal experience. . . .

MR. COOK: I certainly have! I was just a little older than Oscar when I joined the church. I was scared of everyone. I'm still shaky sometimes. But my mother always told me what to do. I looked back that Sunday morning to see if she'd nod her head for me to go to the altar. She did and I did. It's always been that way with me. Religion is a duty. I do it because somebody tells me to. I'm afraid not to.

PASTOR: Sometimes you'd like to throw it all out, but then again. . . .

MR. COOK: Yes, yes. You're the first preacher that ever seemed to understand that. I have been scared to tell the others about it. But what am I to do? You tell me a few things to do and I'll do them.

The pastor had several conferences with Mr. Cook. Oscar was not mentioned again until the third interview when Mr. Cook suggested that Oscar go to a summer camp two weeks hence. "If he goes out there with boys his age and makes good with them, and they like him, then he's old enough to join the church." The father had come to understand the relation between his boy's social maturity and his readiness to make a Christian decision.

Relationships Between Parents

Church memberships can become an acute problem in a home where the mother and father have "solved" their divided church allegiance through inactivity. When a child begins to talk of active church membership, a chronic difficulty between the parents is reactivated. Mr. and Mrs. Gregory became contentious with the pastor about this issue. When the pastor called, their oldest son Paul opened the door, ushered him in, and introduced him to the parents. The parents gave acceptable social responses as the pastor told of Paul's progress in the pastor's class. But both deferred judgment when asked what they thought of Paul's joining the church.

MRS. GREGORY: Well, we have been thinking about it for some time. We just aren't sure what church we will join.

PASTOR: Ah, how long have you been here, Mrs. Gregory?

MRS. GREGORY: Well, I was raised in town. But we moved away years ago. I got away from the church then. We came back here about five years ago.

PASTOR: Which church did you belong to here?

MRS. GREGORY: St. Peter's (*pause*). You see, Mr. Gregory and I were married in your church fifteen years ago. My mother—well, you know how strict families feel. She still wants us to go back to the Catholic Church. . . .

PASTOR: And you, Mr. Gregory?

MR. GREGORY: I tell you, I've been so busy with my business that I haven't given it much thought. Now if the boy really wants to join your church, that's okay with me. I don't know much about it though, and think he should go slow.

PASTOR: I see. I wonder if you've looked at the little booklet that he's been studying. We are anxious that the parents understand it and help teach it to the child.

MR. GREGORY: Oh, no. I get in at seven o'clock and stay on the phone most of the evening.

The result of this direct confrontation was that the mother no longer drove Paul to the bus stop on Sunday morning. When he came with a friend the following month, he explained to the pastor: "My folks don't want to talk any more about the church right now. Maybe I can join later."

Parental anxiety was also acute when the pastor talked with Mrs. Kelly because her thirteen-year-old daughter had said she would join the church when someone else her age did so. Mrs. Kelly began by saying that Paula was very bashful and should not be pushed into a decision. Once this was clarified, Mrs. Kelly said: "Well I'm glad that you don't push us, because I don't like

to—well—it's just that my husband has always been so nice not
to push his religion off on me and I don't want to think I'm push-
ing anything on him."

PASTOR: How's that, Mrs. Kelly?

MRS. KELLY'S MOTHER: You see, my daughter and I are staunch
Baptists. We belong to the Southside Baptist Church. Perhaps we
will take Paula there.

PASTOR: You folks attend there often?

MRS. KELLY'S MOTHER: Well, no, but that's our church home. You
see, we move about so much that we can't really settle down.
(*Southside Church was in another county. The Kelly's were living
in a new $30,000 ranch-style home. Mr. Kelly owned a prospering
dairy. Paula had just shown the pastor "Grandma's room; she stays
here all the time."*)

PASTOR: Ah! We have something to work on here. A staunch Baptist
knows how vital a definite decision is in the life of the child. It may
even quicken your own activity.

MRS. KELLY: Well, I don't know about that. My husband stays home
on Sundays and I want to be with him. That's the important thing.

PASTOR: How about Paula?

MRS. KELLY: You can't push her. She's funny. Doesn't want to discuss things—at least not like this. I know. She wouldn't go down
the aisle with me, I'm sure. It would have to be someone her own
age.

PASTOR: You have discussed this with her?

MRS. KELLY: Oh, no, no. Religion is a very private matter in our
home.

After reporting two failures, it is well to tell of at least one
success. Mr. and Mrs. Emerson were "dormant" Baptists. However, before the disciples' class began, Mrs. Emerson brought
her oldest son Harry to talk with the pastor about church membership. Harry was enrolled in the class, and both Mr. and Mrs.
Emerson began to attend church. When the pastor visited in the
home, Mr. Emerson told of their religious dissension in a joking
manner: "You see, Preacher, here I am a dyed-in-the-wool Baptist, and my wife used to be a Campbellite. Ha! I still laugh about
us going to *the* Christian church when we were courting. I still
suspect she has some of that in her. Of course, I'm not much of a
Baptist these days myself."

MRS. EMERSON: You're enough of a Baptist to get concerned about what your boy is reading in that manual. You sure want to be certain it's *your* doctrine.

PASTOR: Mrs. Emerson, what do you think about all this? Harry's joining a Baptist church.

MRS. EMERSON: Frankly, it's the best thing that has happened to us. I'm ashamed to say it, but although I fuss with my husband about the Christian church, I haven't been much of anything for years. Maybe you better start working on *me*.

The pastor "worked on" all three. Although neither parent has yet accepted any responsibility in the church organization, both are more regular in attendance. When Harry was baptized, Mr. Emerson brought half a dozen friends from his office. He explained to the pastor: "Most of them are Baptists—or Catholics. Now Preacher, I want you to come down to the office and meet some of these folks again. They're about as bad as I have been about going to church. They might as well go here as anywhere else."

The Beginning of Discipline

Pastoral patience is related to children, family, church, and theology in the evangelism of children. In practice, pastoral discipline begins with the pastor. In the above examples, the pastor was willing to set up a schedule of visits to each family represented in the disciples' class and with all children who requested church membership. In interviews with the children, he consistently attempted to relate Christian doctrine to the daily life of the child. He acted as a responsible adult in talking to fathers and mothers on behalf of the children. He did his best to prepare some rocky and confused homes for the cultivation of a new child in the faith. When he could not achieve immediate, visible success, he sought to continue his relationship with the child and the parents until he or someone else in the church could lead them to a definite decision.

These are the patient attitudes that combine love with discipline. These children know that the church expects something of them because the pastor and other important adults have taken a serious and sustained interest in them. Discipline is also possible for these young converts because the pastor sought to relate faith to living, both in his teaching and his personal visits to each home.

This kind of patience did not guarantee complete success. Several of the children made no decision, some of the parents continued to be stumbling blocks, the pastor made mistakes in his counseling that obscured some important motivation in one or more children. When this visitation was finished, the pastor at least knew some of the areas in which he had failed and why he was blocked.

Despite some stony ground, this was a good cultivation of family relationships and childhood motivation for growing Christian faith. But it was only a beginning. The continued care of the pastor, Christian leaders, parents, and friends will be necessary for these babes in Christ to grow to mature manhood in the faith.[29] The challenge of continual growth in grace will be the subject of the next chapter.

[29] For additional material on the evangelism of children, see Yoder, *op. cit.;* Lewis J. Sherrill, *The Opening Doors of Childhood* (New York: The Macmillan Co., 1939); Gaines S. Dobbins, *Winning the Children* (Nashville: Broadman Press, 1953).

7

The Pastoral Care of New Converts

"Grow in grace" is the continual challenge of a new convert. The reformation of a person in Christ must follow the spiritual death of his old self. He is to be diverted from his own instinctive aims into fidelity to the will of Christ. This *re-formation* of personality breaks up the old patterns of life and regroups self-interest toward the central image of the Saviour.

Jesus graphically portrayed this aspect of evangelism in the parable of the sower (Luke 8). When the deeper, entrenched patterns of life are untouched by the gospel, then the Word is as seed on rocky ground. Life sears the first stirrings of a new soul. When the personality is impoverished, the gospel falls as seed on a path. Constant rebuffs and rejections have beaten down the human feelings until a person is flat, colorless, unproductive. Listlessly, the individual watches as other interests eat up a Christian interest he could not sustain. When the personality is disorganized and undisciplined, the Word becomes as seed in a weed patch. The individual cannot integrate his life around the one great purpose of God's will. The seed is choked out by the chaos of unbridled impulses.

The gospel must be cultivated as well as sown. The ever-present peril of the new life is a failure to grow. In American Christianity the major problem is atrophy, a failure to grow, rather than apostasy, a specific repudiation of living faith. The danger is not defiance, but indifference.

Inquirers or converts who drift in their own ways are always in danger of falling back to old patterns of living (Gal. 5:4;

105

Heb. 3:11–16; 10:19–39). Dr. A. T. Robertson made this comment on the problems of recent converts:

Paul frankly warned these new converts (Acts 11:21–23) in this heathen environment of the many tribulations through which they must enter the Kingdom of God. . . . These recent converts from heathenism were ill-informed, were persecuted, had broken family and social ties, greatly needed encouragement if they were to hold out.[1]

The struggle for stability and maturity was perennial in the early church. Legalism "bewitched" the Galatians; the former pride of the Law was replacing the life of faith (Gal. 3:1–5). In the letter to the Hebrews, converts were described as men who wavered in their faith and looked back to a former way of life. To restore their confidence in one greater than Moses, the writer admonished: "But we are not of those who shrink back and are destroyed, but of those who have faith and keep their souls" (Heb. 10:39). The spiritual tepidity and moral turpitude of Asia Minor churches led John to write: "Hold fast what you have, so that no one may seize your crown" (Rev. 3:11; 2:25). Again and again he prefaced the prizes of God with the phrase "to him who conquers." The Christian life is described in the New Testament as a continuing combat: "In all these things we keep on gloriously conquering through Him who loved us" (Rom. 8:37, Williams).

The initial stages of adult conversion are often unstable because the power of a new affection for Christ is confronting the egocentric configurations of a lifetime. Strong emotion may accompany the battle to test and reorient some assumptions of unregenerate living. The challenge is to channel this emotion toward Christian maturity.

In the attempt to stabilize the convert, there are at least two psychological extremes to be avoided. One is the repression of feeling. This is a particular snare of upper middle-class churches. Leaders of such congregations may be uncomfortable in the

---

[1] *Word Pictures in the New Testament* (Nashville: Sunday School Board of the Southern Baptist Convention, 1930), III, 216.

presence of a convert who cries or agonizes over the uprooting of his former way of life.

The other extreme is a fascination with feeling. Some evangelists are so interested in an explosive conversion experience that they ignore a person's subsequent need to replace the pieces of his shattered life. What if the person returns to the same old pattern? Jesus warned that a man whose life is cleansed but vacant is in real peril. The old evil spirit can return, bringing some new ones with him (Luke 11:24–26). Charles Spurgeon observed:

> Some of the most glaring sinners known to me were once members of a church; and were, as I believe, led to make a profession by undue pressure, well-meant but ill judged. . . . It very often happens that the converts that are born in excitement die when the excitement is over. . . . I delight not in the religion which needs or creates a hot head. Give me the Godliness which flourishes upon Calvary rather than upon Vesuvius.[2]

The challenge of new growth lays heavy claims upon the church and the convert. Exhortations, examples, and criteria for growth are found throughout the New Testament (Acts 11:23; Heb. 3:13–14; Jude 20; 1 Peter 2:5–8, 10). Pauline letters contain numerous references to a firm stand in the faith through continual growth in grace (1 Cor. 15:1–2; 2 Cor. 1:24; Gal. 6:1; Phil. 1:27; 3:12–16; Eph. 3:14–19; Rom. 8:18–39; Phil. 2:1–13).

Costly Grace or Cheap Admission?

How well does the modern church fulfil this mission of personal reconstruction? An answer to this question involves all the ministries of the church and goes far beyond the present subject of evangelism. But evangelists have some responsibility for the beginnings of growth, the structuring of commitment into creative channels of fellowship, service, devotion, and study. This chapter will examine some institutionalized methods by which converts are encouraged toward church membership: the evangelistic sermon and invitation, the communicants' class, and pas-

[2] *Op. cit.,* pp. 12–14.

toral counseling. These will be evaluated by the biblical teaching that salvation reconciles men to God and to each other in the household of God (Eph. 2).

Admission to full membership in Episcopal, Lutheran, and Reformed churches has come traditionally through communicants' classes. Instruction in faith and order are required. Unfortunately, this requirement can become an impersonal, unimaginative procedure which lacks spontaneity and commitment.

An Episcopal professor of pastoral care, Dr. Reuel Howe, wrote in the October, 1961 "Newsletter" of the Institute for Advanced Pastoral Studies:

Preparation for church membership is one function of the ministry that needs re-examination and overhauling. . . . The loss to the church of those once admitted to membership is an indication that not all is well. Of those who remain, some maintain only a formal relationship with the church; others have a moralistic understanding of Christianity and think they have to earn their membership by being good instead of depending upon the love and forgiveness of God. Others substitute the local church for the Kingdom, and work and pray and give for its success rather than for the Kingdom. Others leave it to the clergy to carry on the church's ministry, and, in so doing contribute to the disease of clericalism, a disease that overstresses the role of the ordained members and confines the activity of the church's ministry to what they do. As a result of all these conditions, the church does not influence the world as it should.

Many Baptist, Christian, and Methodist groups, continuing the frontier tradition, receive members on the basis of their spontaneous response to a public invitation. Personal decision is encouraged, but this method may also become routine and impersonal. In recent years a major defect has been a lack of attention to the candidate for baptism after his public profession.

A president of the Southern Baptist Convention, Dr. Herschel Hobbs, told the faculty of the Southern Baptist Seminary: "We have equated salvation with regeneration, but regeneration is only one part of salvation. We have neglected dedication, sanctification, and consecration. We have majored on bigness, not on depth. We have 'dipped 'em and dropped 'em.' "

In addition to the dangers of ecclesiastical routine and personal neglect, both liturgical and nonliturgical admission procedures are threatened by secularism. Church membership is a socially accepted route to respectability in America today. As Will Herberg has persuasively argued in *Protestant-Catholic-Jew,* religious affiliation is the American sign of "belonging" which is substituted for earlier adherence to an Old World culture. To join a church in many sections of a city is to be "in with the right people." [3] "Popular religion" has become a secularized substitute for sacrificial commitment to historic Christian faith.[4]

In *The Cost of Discipleship* Dietrich Bonhoeffer accused the church of preaching "cheap grace." American churches might also be accused of practicing cheap admission. Popular religion has removed dedication, suffering, and humility from the gospel; secular success standards have taken fellowship and discipline out of church membership.

To fulfil the commission of personal reconstruction in a secular society, the church must offer both spontaneous grace and personal discipline to new converts. Individual decision and group fellowship must be made one in the body of Christ. The best elements of the public invitation and the communicants' class must be combined.

The Invitation to Commitment

For the sake of spontaneity and personal commitment, liturgical communions should turn to the public invitation to Christian discipleship. This can be combined with personal sharing through the "talk-back" sessions which have been used enthusiastically by pastors from the Institute for Advanced Pastoral Studies. In an evening group meeting, hearers of the Sunday morning message raise questions with the minister or make comments to the

[3] Gerhard Lenski has studied the influence of the religious factor upon social position, family, and political attitudes. *The Religious Factor* (New York: Doubleday & Co., 1961).

[4] Cf. Louis Schneider and Sanford Dornbusch, *Popular Religion: American Inspirational Literature* (Chicago: University of Chicago Press, 1958); Martin Marty, *The New Shape of American Religion* (New York: Harper & Brothers, 1959).

group. These discussions may have the mood of "what the gospel means to me." When such a feeling is present, an inquirer may wish to ask what the gospel could mean to him also. Why not invite those who have not made a commitment to meet with the pastor after the "talk-back" session?

Denominations in the frontier tradition should be more imaginative in their public invitations and more insistent upon inquirer's classes as a part of the initial commitment to Christ.

In some churches the spontaneous invitations of a hundred years ago have become a modern ritual: "If there is a person here who does not know Christ as Saviour . . . ." In addition to some such regularly repeated formula, this kind of invitation has other marks of ritualism. It is connected neither to the body of the sermon nor to the feelings of the audience. A narrow routine is further entrenched by the singing of a specialized group of "invitation hymns." [5] One of the favorites is "Just As I Am." Dr. Wayne Oates once suggested to a group of ministerial students that they sing this song at the beginning of a worship service. One student pastor tried this and then called on a deacon to lead in prayer. The deacon immediately dismissed the congregation with a benediction!

Evangelistic sermons, invitations, and hymns need to broaden their appeal and specify their objectives. One way to avoid ritualization is to select texts from a wide variety of biblical subjects that call for different kinds of commitment. Some messages make demands upon family life, some ask for a change of civic attitudes, others require a public confession of Christ for the first time. The converted and the unconverted can be challenged to Christian growth when a year's pulpit ministry contains more than a last-minute rehashing of popular revival themes.

Stereotyped phrases can also be overcome through an invitation that is consistent with the theme of the sermon and the re-

---

[5] In some hymnals it would be difficult to find appropriate hymns on commitment to Christian living in the family, church, or community. For example, the *Baptist Hymnal* contains selections on Christ's forgiveness of men but none on the forgiving spirit of man for man. The theme of fellowship in the church is not stressed in "invitation hymns." See "Topical Index," *Baptist Hymnal* (Nashville: Convention Press, 1956), p. 555.

sponse of the audience. The endings of many modern sermons would not be so weak and repetitious if they were filled with power and were sensitive to the moving of God's Spirit among the listeners. How long has it been since a modern sermon concluded with a cry from the audience: "Brethren, what shall we do?" (Acts 2:37).

At Pentecost the audience response was the invitation. The Holy Spirit concluded Peter's speech in Cornelius' house through the open rejoicing of the Gentiles (Acts 10:44–48). Stephen's sermon led to a riot (Acts 7:54–60). Paul's address to the Antioch synagogue ended with a request from the Jews that he tell them more the next Saturday (Acts 13:42–43). Each of these messages was a challenge to Christian commitment—but each in a different way and with a varied response.

The appeal for an initial commitment to Christ should not sound as an afterthought of messages on a variety of themes; it should be the climax of a sermon built upon an evangelistic appeal.

Does this mean that public invitations should be confined to periodic revival meetings? No. Pastoral preaching calls for evangelistic messages, just as revival sermons demand a variety of responses. It is unscriptural to say: "I preach Christ as Saviour in a revival and Christ as Lord later on." How can Christ save a man's "soul" without dominating his life? Jesus said: "You shall love the Lord your God with all your heart, and with all your soul, and with all your mind . . . (and) you shall love your neighbor as yourself" (Matt. 22:37–39). He did not say: "Love your Saviour today with your soul and make him Lord of your life tomorrow."

Those who separate Saviour-Lord are attempting to disjoin man and God's message. "We cannot be justified freely through faith alone without at the same time living holily. For these gifts are connected, as if by an indissoluble tie, so that he who attempts to sever them does in a manner tear Christ in pieces." [6] The biblical call to salvation would "reconcile us to God in one

---

[6] John Calvin, *Commentary on the Epistles of Paul the Apostle to the Corinthians* (Grand Rapids: Wm. B. Eerdmans Publishing Co., 1948), I, 93.

body" and make us "fellow citizens with the saints." The call of God is a call to walk worthy of him in every aspect of life (Eph. 2–6).

The inseparability of commitment and growth can be demonstrated through special series of revival messages as well as through the weekly messages to a local congregation. A revival series can include messages on (1) the lordship of Christ in the church as a precondition of revival; (2) the lordship of self *versus* a Saviour; (3) the cost of discipleship; (4) the meaning of Christian life in the family; and (5) the responsibility of saved people for the redemption of society. Messages on sin and forgiveness, thought and decision were preached in one rural church. The most frequent comment of the listeners was: "Never before in a revival have we been challenged this deeply."

Fellowship for Discipleship

Sermons may create the expectation of growth and fellowship; many persons may shake hands with a "joiner." But after a convert has made his public commitment, how does the church help him to grow in grace, to be knit together into the body of Christ? [7]

Face-to-face groups are the means by which the church has most often schooled converts. Halford Luccock's commentary on Jesus' appointment of the apostles (Mark 3:13–19) was: "All the great movements in Christianity have been based on the training of small groups." [8] Some modern examples of fellowship for discipleship are Sunday school classes, inquirer's classes, and person-centered groups which meet for prayer or personal therapy.

The Sunday school class.—How may a Sunday school class have significance for new Christians? If the teacher lectures, it will add little more than assorted biblical information. But if there is participation through discussion, the convert will have opportunity to see how other people feel about questions of reli-

[7] Ephesians 4:11–16.
[8] George A. Buttrick (ed.), *The Interpreter's Bible* (New York: Abingdon Press, 1951), VII, 686.

gion in life. He also can test his own ideas with a sympathetic group that is controlled by a concern for the accurate biblical witness in modern application.

In one Adult Bible class the teacher took ten or fifteen minutes to summarize the Sunday school lesson and to point to relevant issues that it raised for modern life.

Several questions were suggested, such as "Do you think that your brother would have been wise to do as Hosea did about his marriage?" or "How can we understand the pastoral Epistles when we endure no persecution?" For the next half hour there was a lively exchange of views between husbands and wives, liberals and conservatives, lawyers, businessmen, and barbers. Doubts and convictions were openly expressed. In another session on Genesis, questions came up about the time of creation. Forty-year-old people admitted after class that this was their first discussion of science and religion without fear of condemnation.

Among the thirty people that sat in the semicircle of this class each Sunday were some who were making their first decisions about the Christian faith. One chemical engineer had talked with the teacher about science and religion when he was first invited to the class. A year later, when he made a profession of faith, he said: "Thanks for that talk at home and for those open discussions in class. It took away the guilt I had about my doubts."

Personal relations were also developed through a monthly class meeting in a member's home. This was an opportunity for business and fellowship. "Group captains" reported on their contacts with new members and questions were raised about absentees. Prospects for the church and the class were suggested and assigned for visitation. After half an hour the meeting broke up for refreshments and small groups of people formed for socializing or continuing Sunday's discussion. It looked so smooth, but it took some planning. Just to please his wife, one man who had not been to church in twenty years attended a class meeting. He soon found that these people had some interests like his own and that he was welcomed. It took months for his old resentments to diminish, but through these meetings they did begin to break.

From this combination of open discussion, organized fellowship, and continual visitation by class members came a higher percentage of new members for the church than from any other Adult class. Of course this kind of group can develop into a clique, but that risk is worth running when the leader hears an executive say: "This is the only crowd we can go out with where drinks are not served."

The inquirer's class.—The fellowship and instruction of Sunday school can prepare individuals for participation in an inquirer's class. This group should be open to men and women who have already made or who are interested in making an open declaration of faith in Christ. In order that the discussion may concentrate on the interests of specific age groups, a separate class or individual conference should be offered to older children and adolescents. Some churches offer these group discussions several times a year; others link them to a revival. A group may begin when six or more are interested in church membership.

Churches that require instruction before reception of a convert for church membership will find that small group discussions will help candidates in many ways. This will also be true for those who are voted into church membership and then attend a "new members' class" as part of their orientation to the church and its membership. In his leadership of such a group, Dr. John Boyle [9] found that converts needed help in at least four areas of faith and life. These will be documented from his work as associate pastor with sixty new members of a large, lower middle- and middle-class urban church.

The first need of the convert is an adequate interpretation of his Christian experience. Dr. Boyle found that this was especially necessary for those who joined the church under intense emotion. After a "mountaintop experience," they were jolted by the descent into everyday realities. Their intense spirituality had to be teamed up with slow-moving reality.[10]

[9] John Boyle, "Group Dynamics in the Care of New Members" (Master's thesis, Southern Baptist Theological Seminary, Louisville, Ky., 1955).

[10] Myron Madden, "The Crisis of Becoming a Christian," *Pastoral Psychology*, May, 1951, p. 31.

This was demonstrated in the profession of faith by a nineteen-year-old girl. She felt much guilt over the premarital sexual relations which she had had with her steady boy friend. During her initial conversion experience she experienced a sense of God's forgiveness. She plunged into church activities as a way to atone for her sins. About two months after her conversion, she came to the associate pastor questioning the genuineness of her religious feelings. Recently she had not kept up the pace of church activity. Her explanation was: "After all the excitement of the revival, I feel quite let down. I guess I need to find out how all of what has happened to me fits into the daily routine of life. After all, you can't go to revival meetings forever."

A second need of new members is for recognition by Christian people who seem important to them. Now that they are fellow citizens in God's kingdom, they want to know and be known by others in this local fellowship of God's people.

To be important to others does not mean that these new converts must have a place of pre-eminence. It does mean that they are to have a place which is recognized as important. For example, a mentally retarded woman was eager to help in her new members' class. She could not compete in conversation, but she could arrive at the meeting before others to arrange chairs, place flowers, or give out literature. A smile and a word of commendation from the leader and others was her reward. She had a place that was important to those who were important to her.

Recognition in the group extends beyond a place of service. It also includes an interest in the ordinary affairs of living. Members of the class are cheered when someone asks about the health of their children or the success of their work. Mothers share their worries about sick children; fathers discuss economic conditions; young people share their plans for the future.

A third need of new members is personal unburdening. This may be expressed in a Christian fellowship that is a gathered community of sinners. The intimacy of a small class of fifteen [11] new members encourages sharing. At times, converts may need to confess their hostilities and temptations. Some need comfort

[11] This was the size of one group during the year when this study was made.

in the loss of affection within their own family. One woman told in quiet desperation of the abuse she suffered from her husband. As others contributed to the discussion, she began to understand more about the reasons for her husband's actions and her own attitudes. This insight eased tension in the home.

The fourth need is for instruction in Christian living. Part of this need can be met through the transmission of information with which the new members can relate themselves to the life and ministry of the church.[12] But the need must also be met on an individual basis. The converts need personal guidance to handle some of the more "knotty" problems of everyday living and the entrenched personality patterns of a lifetime.

Person-centered groups.—When any member of the church is "tied in knots" by personal conflicts, he needs a more intimate fellowship than has been previously described. This need will be imperative for new converts who confront changing demands on their old way of living and their old way of looking at themselves and others. How can they be reformed in the image of Christ?

An answer to this is the face-to-face group of ten or twelve people who meet weekly to discuss their way of life and thought. Some of these groups have been described in John Casteel's *Spiritual Renewal Through Personal Groups*. One fellowship began with a desire to understand the Bible. Individuals wrote sentences or a page of their own views on biblical themes such as sin and salvation. One or two of these were read to the group. People were soon asking the "foolish" questions that had bothered them for years. The members were gripped by a desire to see how faith really applied to their own lives. Several of these weekly groups came together with other persons in the church for a monthly meeting to explore the meaning of such familiar phrases as "getting close to God," "faith," "love," or "eternal life." It developed an honest probing for personal answers.

---

[12] Some topics for discussion may be found at the end of this chapter. For adults coming from an urban, secular culture, Albert Mollegen's *Christianity and Modern Man* (Indianapolis: Bobbs-Merrill Co., 1961), will be most instructive.

Another type of group developed into the Church of the Saviour in Washington, D. C. The fifty-five members and two hundred worshipers of this congregation were led by their Baptist
pastor, Gordon Cosby, to divide into three groups for nurture,
service, and evangelism. Each group carries out its task as part
of the total church program. Each group meets weekly for supper, devotions, and discussion. The nonchurch members usually
enter a discussion group on Christian growth. All discussion
groups converge at 9:40 P.M. for fellowship and refreshments
in the old house that is their church building. The church also
operates "The Potter's Wheel," a coffee shop where members
meet people attracted by the atmosphere of an "Espresso house"
and talk to them about Christianity and life.

Other types of person-centered groups meet for prayer and
personal therapy. Usually a chapter from a book on prayer or
devotion is studied. The members then discuss their own feelings
and experiences. In the Central Methodist Church, Evansville,
Indiana, nine members of a prayer group took psychological
tests before and after a year of weekly group discussion. Minnesota Multiphasic Inventory Tests indicated that six of the members showed definite personality improvement from neurotic depression, hysterical or hypochondriacal reaction, paranoid reaction, or former psychosis.[13]

The above mentioned examples are from urban churches.
What about a rural membership? Pastor William Salyers organized a discussion group before each revival service in his rural
Indiana church. About eight persons came for an hour each
night. On the first night, the pastor read 2 Chronicles 7:14
and asked the people how personal relations might be improved
so that God's power would move through the church to unsaved
persons. A deacon asked: "How can I invite others when my own
daughter won't come to church any more?" He began to cry.
Others in the group tried to comfort him. In doing so, they began
to share their own frustrations in relation to the church. Several
people described how limited they were in persuading their
family or friends to be active in the church.

[13] Personal correspondence with Pastor Robert Glass (Oct. 18, 1961).

On the following evening, one person opened the discussion by asking if suicide were a sin. Several months before, a prominent church member had killed himself. His wife, who had been active, now excluded herself from the church. Here was another personal barrier that had to be conquered. By the end of the week, those in attendance had gained so much that they requested such discussion in preparation for future revivals. What would happen if these groups were not only formed before a revival for church members, but also after the meeting for inquirers and converts?

If a pastor or church leader [14] is interested in developing new members through any of the three types of groups which have been described above, he should study some of these practical and readable books:

DAY, LEROY JUDSON. *Dynamic Christian Fellowship*. Philadelphia: Judson Press, 1960.

MILLER, PAUL M. *Group Dynamics in Evangelism*. Scottdale, Pa.: Herald Press, 1958.

MUNRO, HARRY C. *Fellowship Evangelism Through Church Groups*. St. Louis: Bethany Press, 1951.

CASTEEL, JOHN. *Spiritual Renewal Through Personal Groups*. New York: Association Press, 1957.

MOSER, LESLIE. *Counseling: A Modern Emphasis in Religion*. Englewood Cliffs, N. J.: Prentice-Hall, Inc., 1962. (A verbatim example of group counseling may be found on pp. 322–38.)

After studying these, a pastor may wish to participate in some group experience. This will give him instruction and a feeling for the processes of interpersonal involvement. Opportunity for such participation may come through clinical training courses, retreats, or short-term workshops offered for the clergy.[15]

---

[14] Laymen who have had experience in group relations often may be the leaders of person-centered groups. Mr. Bill Wigglesworth of Cynthiana, Kentucky, has led several of these groups which were formed out of members or prospects for the Adult Sunday school department of which he is superintendent.

[15] Outstanding workshops which stress group experience include the Department of Religion, Baptist Hospital, Winston-Salem, North Carolina; Institute of Religion, Texas Medical Center, Houston, Texas; Institute for Advanced Pastoral Studies, Bloomfield Hills, Michigan.

These face-to-face groups are vital for the reception of members into Protestant churches. The method and philosophy of sharing and confession can personalize a traditional communicants' class. A required class of instruction and fellowship can seal the commitment which an inquirer made public during a hymn of invitation. Denominations that are burdened by a growing list of missing and inactive members may find that discipline and righteousness are deepened through the shared experiences and instruction of these groups which precede church membership.[16]

In the Church of the Saviour, a year of study and participation precedes church membership. Those who are received into membership must make an annual recommitment to the congregation. The minimum discipline of this church calls for "(1) daily prayer; (2) weekly worship; (3) daily study of the Scriptures; (4) membership in a fellowship group or participation in the educational program; (5) tithing, as a minimum stewardship program; (6) daily expression of Christian love in redeeming service." [17] This kind of discipline can be required when the church offers instruction, fellowship, and sharing in the body of Christ.

The Family of New Members

The fellowship of Christian groups strengthens new converts in the "household of faith." [18] But what of the intimate life of a family group? How may it be a source of grace for new life in Christ?

The pattern, rapidity, and stability of personality changes are influenced by significant people in the individual's private world

[16] For example, if the Southern Baptist Convention continues to produce as many spiritually dead as spiritually alive members (according to C. E. Matthews and the "First Church" study), the meaning of church membership will steadily decline. At the present time, some of the most embarrassing and vicious attacks upon Christian leaders in the South come from citizens who are nominal members of a church.

[17] John Casteel, *Spiritual Renewal Through Personal Groups* (New York: Association Press, 1957), p. 171.

[18] Lenski's study, *op. cit.*, of the religious factor in Detroit families showed that active Protestants valued friendships outside the family more than family ties, pp. 220–21.

of home, friends, and work. The psychiatric studies of Dr. Nathan Ackerman [19] and Dr. Warren Brodey [20] have shown how family patterns influence individual behavior. In the Family Study Project at the National Institute of Mental Health, a change in parental attitudes and actions might cause a psychotic daughter to make rapid gains toward health.[21]

Similar investigations of recent converts might demonstrate the reviving or retarding influence of family relationships. Some of the examples in the previous discussion of small groups point to the importance of husband-wife and parent-child attitudes for Christian living. A wife was able to bring her resentful husband to a Sunday school fellowship where he might re-examine his impression of churchmen. In a revival discussion group a father began to see dimly his own responsibility for his daughter's indifference to the church.

Sampling of a denominational group, such as Fairchild and Wynn's interviews with 845 Presbyterian families, demonstrates the present gap between the church and family relationships. Just over half of the parents in the sampling were able to relate personal life to Christian faith. Yet only half of the pastors held regular interviews with the parents of children about to be baptized.[22]

How may pastoral evangelists strengthen the family's godly influence and combat attitudes of family members that would weaken a convert?

In the example of the deacon who spoke of his daughter in a pre-revival meeting, the pastor followed up the discussion by several private conferences with the father. The father soon admitted that all was not well between himself and his domineering wife. He had stood by while she had insisted on an elaborate church wedding for the daughter. The daughter had protested this because many persons in the community knew that she was

[19] *Psychodynamics of Family Life* (New York: Basic Books, Inc., 1958).
[20] "Some Family Operations and Schizophrenia," *A.M.A. Archives of General Psychiatry*, I, 379–402.
[21] Murray Bowen, "The Role of the Father in Families with a Schizophrenic Patient."
[22] Roy Fairchild and John Wynn, *Families in the Church: a Protestant Survey* (New York: Association Press, 1961), pp. 10, 174, 231.

with child. As on many previous occasions, the father was passive while the mother triumphed over the provoked daughter. Six months after the wedding, the mother was mortified to find herself a grandmother. She heaped reproaches upon her daughter for "disgracing the family name." Furious that she had not been told of the pregnancy, she cried: "How can I ever hold up my head and sing in the choir after that big wedding!" The daughter shouted: "Then you'll not need to worry, because you'll never see me in church again so long as you are there!"

When the pastor talked to the mother, she played the role of martyr. When he talked to the daughter, she said that she had asked God for forgiveness, loved her baby and husband, and would like to return to church with her husband, but not while her mother could stare at her from the choir.

It will take much work and prayer for the daughter and mother to confess their mutual sins to each other. As a first step, does the father have the courage to confront his wife with her attitudes? to tell her why the daughter would not reveal her pregnancy? to confess that he had acquiesced to all this and was guilty of a lack of responsible participation in family decisions?

An investigation of family relationships and the growth of a convert would need to consider the impact of individual members of the family upon each other. One of the many problems to be considered would be the place of the father in Christian nurture. In the Bible and in the Church Fathers, the man was dominant, but in the modern American Protestant family, women are more active in church work.[23] Although the father seems to be less active in organized Christianity, Ernest Ligon's "Home Dynamics Study" indicates that the father sets the moral tone of the family, even though it is often done in a clumsy manner.[24]

How may the traditional dominance of the father in moral affairs be related to the maturation of a new Christian?

A thirteen-year-old boy made a profession of faith after a very troubled year in the school and community. He had begun to run

[23] *Ibid.*, p. 195.
[24] *Parent Roles: His and Hers* (Schenectady, N. Y.: Ernest Ligon, 1959), pp. 7–9.

with an older, "wild" crowd. Six months before his profession, his father had talked in distress with the pastor. The father confessed his own moral delinquencies and took responsibility for his son's imitation of them. For his son's sake, he said, he was driven to make a decision for Christ which he might otherwise have postponed until he was too old to enjoy "helling around." "But," he added, "by then I'd be too feeble to influence my boy, so now's the time."

After his public decision, the father was closely watched by the son. When three months had passed, the boy asked his father how he kept going when his old friends laughed at him so much. The father replied:

"Boy, we've had some good times together, but lately I've been seeing in you some things that I'd put off caring for in myself. Now I'm not fit to preach to you, and am no good at that anyway. But you asked me, so I'm telling you, don't wait till my age to shed a wild crowd and trust in God."

The father got up and left the room. Three months later, the son made his profession of faith. Since then, he has asked his father such questions as:

"Dad, how did you tell your friends that you couldn't go some places with them? . . . Hey, Dad, how do you answer the men who think you're a sissy for having religion?"

Individual Pastoral Care

Every resource of the Christian community is needed for the development of new Christians. Sermons, group discussions, and family relations can be invitations and resources for growth. Individual attention must be a part of every evangelistic effort. In a revival meeting the pastor and evangelist can personalize public invitations by inviting inquirers to meet individually with them. By having several conferences the evangelist can strengthen the inquirer and determine when he should be encouraged to apply for church membership. He and the pastor may decide that the inquirer is ready for a class in fellowship and instruction for baptism and church membership. In any case, the evangelist can be a minister of reconciliation between the inquirer and the Christian fellowship.

One evangelist had such an opportunity when he was pastor of a youth camp. A twelve-year-old girl responded to his public invitation for discipleship on the last night of his messages to the youngsters. She was crying at the time and continued to weep for several minutes after the pastor led her to his office for consultation. At first she would only say that she wanted to be saved. After a few questions she admitted that she came because she feared death. Why did she fear death? Had anyone in her family died recently? The girl confessed that a favorite uncle died two months ago. Since then her thoughts had been of death and eternity.

Because it was growing late, the pastor suggested a second conference on the following morning. The girl returned in the morning and talked about the relation of faith to daily living, including a better understanding of death and eternal life. After interpreting Christian grief to her, the pastor asked, "Is there anything else we should talk about now?"

"Yes," she said. "I am an adopted child. It's bothered me some since I found out. I wonder who my natural parents are. But, well, I must say that I'm happy with my adopted parents (*pause*). I feel better now. I just wanted to tell somebody who would understand."

When the girl returned to her home community, the camp pastor wrote to her pastor and to her. The minister in her community talked to the girl and she wrote her camp pastor after several weeks:

Dear Rev. L.:

How are you? Fine I hope. I accepted Christ publicly Sunday morning. . . . Sunday night I told the church in a few words why I accepted Christ. Brother L., I don't know how to thank you for all you've done for me. If you ever get out toward M-town Church, stop over and visit me. It's hard to find, so I drew a map for you to my house (map enclosed).

Pastoral evangelists report that these personal conferences and letters often begin a lifetime of correspondence. People do not forget a minister who has a personal interest in their lives.

Public invitations in a local church can be personal when deacons, elders, or other church leaders greet those who respond. Deacons of the Third Baptist Church, St. Louis, meet each in-

quirer during the invitation hymn. There are mutual greetings
and questions before the prospective member is introduced to the
congregation. This avoids the mechanical method of handing
prospects a slip of paper with hurried instructions to fill it out
before the hymn is finished.

In churches that invite inquirers to speak to the pastor or to a
deacon about membership, and have no hymn of invitation, the
process of reception is made more personal by the assignment of
a mature church member as sponsor for each person in a communicants' class. In the Fifth Avenue Presbyterian Church, New
York City, representatives of various church organizations
serve as sponsors for new members. These sponsors are asked to
introduce the new members to the church and its people. Three
months after the member joins, the sponsor is asked for a report on the life of this new member. Two other reports are requested from a sponsor by the pastor during the first year of
membership.[25]

In his first days as a church member, a person may be very
sensitive to pastoral attention. If neglected now, he may become
cynical about the church which promised so much a few weeks
before. If ministered to, he will always remember this as firm
testimony of the church's concern.

A middle-aged businessman, Mr. M, stood outside a hospital
room while his partner, Mr. C, lay inside with a heart attack. Mr.
C's pastor came, spoke to the family and had prayer with Mr. C.
As the pastor left the room, Mr. M walked down the hall with
him and said:

"I—I wish I had some pastor on whom I could call if I were
in trouble. I saw what you did. It meant so much to C's family.
But my family—"

The pastor asked about Mr. M's religious history. He discovered that early poverty and later business success had occupied
all of Mr. M's attention. But now he was slowing down and
wanted to take stock of himself. Later, the pastor visited Mr. M
at home. After several conferences, Mr. M made a profession of

[25] S. W. Powell, *Where Are the Converts?* (Nashville: Broadman Press,
1958), p. 124.

faith and his wife moved her membership to the same church.

Within a month Mr. M was kept in bed with a stomach ulcer. When the pastor called on him, Mr. M began to reveal some of the strains of his business. The fear of poverty in the 1930's still haunted him. His great battle for faith was centered about this searing memory of adolescence. Could he stop acquiring more money and property and take some time for his family and his church? As things stood now, he played golf or fished just as he worked—compulsively, tensely waiting to count up his gains. "I've got to break this!" he said.

As the pastor left, Mrs. M followed him to the car and said, "My husband has always needed a man to talk to. I'm glad that you're coming to see him again in a few days. I guess we just didn't know that a pastor could help us this way. And so many of the people have called. We're not used to it—ah, in fact, M wishes no one knew he was in bed, but it has to be, I guess. Anyway, thanks."

A year later, Mr. M was appointed to the church finance committee. It was reported to the pastor that Mr. M told a tightfisted business associate: "Listen J, I know all that stuff about the church, but ours is different. There are people up there who care about us. They came through when we needed help. I'm going to do my part for them, and I want you to do the same."

Mr. M needed more than a group ministry to realign his patterns of thought. Without an exploration of his fears and loneliness from the pastor, he might have become the watchdog of the finance committee, always warning of depression-to-come. With new understanding, however, he was a warm supporter of his church.

The pastor and church leader's ministry to converts should be both a routine and a crisis ministry. As a customary courtesy, the pastor should call on each new member in his home. A visit from other church leaders will give a husband comradeship with another man of his own age, or a wife the opportunity to discuss with the chairman of a woman's organization the ways in which the church cares for children. These visits show new members and their families that the church does care.

With this assurance, new members feel free to call on the pastor or other church members in a time of crisis. Sometimes a pastor complains because a new member is in trouble and no one has told him. Who would? He knows no member of the family, has never been in the home, and no church officer has made it a point to be individually acquainted with this member and his family. Is it any wonder that some converts suffer in silence and drift away?

The Channels of Grace

An evangelistic hymn of this century contains the refrain, "make me a channel of blessing." This chapter has explored some channels of Christian growth. These must flow together.

Just as public invitations and communicants' classes can be criticized as routine and impersonal by themselves, so may pastoral counseling be censored as an individual experience which is isolated from the communion of the church. The ministries of the church cannot be conducted in the absolute professional secrecy which characterizes a psychiatrist's office. New converts cannot be built up apart from involvement in the lives of many people. Some of the problems which a convert shares with a pastor must be mentioned by the pastor to responsible church leaders who can minister to those who are involved.

The actions of the pastor in calling upon one family member may be a sign that another member, or friend, has spelled out the actual relationships of this home. In small communities, a pastor or church official cannot drive down the road without notice. Wherever his car is parked, conversation will gather. Should this conversation be hidden or condemned as gossip? In a Christian fellowship it should be redeemed. Neurotic and cultural defenses must be broken by the loving concern of the community gathered in Christ.

The channel of grace may be the shared experience of an inquirer's class or a prayer group. It may be the aggressive ministry of one man to another for the sake of his child who is a babe in Christ. At times it will be a deeper exploration of buried feelings under the guidance of a pastoral counselor. Whatever the means, the need is for church leaders who can lead group discussions to deeper levels of personal insight and sharing and individuals from the privacy of individual consultation into a shared relationship of trust and intimacy with a group of fellow Christians. These relationships can be the channels of blessing for a convert and a source of revival for the total church.

Psychologically and theologically, the nurture of new members requires a reorientation of isolated church life and individualized pastoral counseling. The ministry of church and pastor must be renewed in fellowship, in sharing, in communication. This is an essential aspect of evangelism, for the common life of Christians is the cradle of the convert. It is here that he learns the quality of relationships which distinguish those who follow Christ. Fellowship between man and man is upon the same basis as fellowship between man and God (Matt. 18:21–35). The appeal of God is made through human representatives (2 Cor. 5:20 to 6:10). In love for one another we imitate God (Eph. 5:1–2). Our ability to understand and sympathize brings conviction to the hearts of unbelievers (1 Cor. 14:23–25).[26]

However, the fellowship which channels God's grace is not the source of salvation in itself. The source is Christ revealed in his Spirit (Eph. 4:13–16; 2 Cor. 13:14; 1 Cor. 12–14). His life determines the quality of our relationships. His power is manifest in the fellowship of brethren whose relations are transformed in quality and significance through the shared gift of his grace. These transformed relationships may be seen as the "fruit of the spirit" (Gal. 5:22 to 6:5).

The church is not a collection of individuals who give assent to certain propositions, but a partnership of those who share common devotion to Christ. It is characterized by the sharing of suffering and the strengthening of those in trouble (2 Cor. 1:5–7; 1 Cor. 12:26; 1 Peter 5:9–10; James 5:13–18; Rom. 15:1; Gal. 6:1–6). The priesthood of believers describes this ministry of Christians to each other.[27] The nurture of new converts is a re-

[26] Thornton, *op. cit.*, pp. 40 ff.
[27] T. W. Manson, *Ministry and Priesthood: Christ's and Ours* (Richmond: John Knox, 1958), pp. 35–72.

sponsibility of all who participate in the body of Christ. Individual reformation is built upon redemptive relationships, divine and human.

Church Polity for Disciplined Growth

Pastoral counsel, inquirer's classes, evangelistic sermons, and personal relationships can set the pattern for Christian growth. To strengthen the new convert and the church against superficial routines and eroding secularism, the frontier requirements for membership should again become church polity:

(1) public invitations to discipleship;
(2) group instruction and fellowship of candidates;
(3) guidance and examination of the candidate by the pastor;
(4) testimony of Christian faith and experience by the candidate to the church membership;
(5) vote by the congregation or session in business meeting to accept or reject the candidate on the basis of his group participation, counsel with the pastor, personal testimony, and recommendation by reliable witnesses;
(6) public reception of the candidate through baptism or transfer of church membership;
(7) sponsorship of the new member by a mature Christian for at least one year.

The Social Class of the Church and the Convert

With all this preparation for new members, a church may still find that some people "just don't fit in." Actually, there are large segments of the population that would not be at ease in any one congregation. The social class of the convert is an important factor in his acceptance of, and by, the church of his choice.

Clues to status are noticeable in the first greeting of ushers to a visitor. In one upper-class church, a husband and wife stand at the entrance to the sanctuary and welcome newcomers. Their manner, dress, and phrases, such as "We are most pleased to welcome you," are signs of a gracious, reserved constituency. In a middle-class church an usher greets each person with a bulletin of the worship service and asks where he would like to be seated.

The usher does not wear the fresh carnation which distinguishes the upper-class host, and his suit is several years old. In a lower-class church, several men stand on the steps of the church and look for prospective members. They warmly take the hand of any visitor, grin broadly, and introduce him to several of the church leaders before he is led into the "auditorium." Their hands are rough and their ties are wide. People are made welcome with a slap on the back.

Inquirers may be vaguely aware that something is wrong and, with no knowledge of social strata, may accuse the church of incorrect theology or spirit. For example, a lower-class man who joined an upper-class church that remained in a transitional neighborhood, left after several months with the remark: "Broadway's not on the ball for the Lord!" He found warm acceptance in a lower middle-class church where, as he put it: "They *show* that they want you."

In contrast, young couples who are rising fast in suburbia may become dissatisfied with the "straight-laced" morality of their Methodist or Baptist parents. They may be particularly anxious to be in a church that accepts "social drinking," for they see drinking as a sign of acceptance at cocktail parties and company banquets. It usually will not be difficult for them to find a suburban church that secures members on the basis of social cues that are never discussed in specific terms, just as the church of their parents continues its appeal to the small-town virtues of a previous century.

When a church recruits members from more than one social group, it is difficult to be all things to all men. But recognition of a person's class may aid in drawing him into the fellowship. He may be assigned a sponsor who has a similar background. If he is brought into contact with enough small groups in the church, he will soon find some people of like interests. For example, a plasterer joined a church in which 50 per cent of the adults were college graduates. He was so uncomfortable in social gatherings that he loudly proclaimed to the pastor at a church banquet: "Well, I'm not like some of these other guys. You see, I *work* for a living." He was miserable until a skilled machine operator invited him and his family to his home for Christmas dinner. Here the family met people with whom they were comfortable. The men were foremen and skilled workmen who had lived in the area before it became a fashionable suburban settlement. By staying with the church they provided a place for other people of similar interest.

Since new members find their primary identification with the church through face-to-face contacts, social cues are most important in Sunday school classes, men's and women's organizations. Persons of similar interests will naturally "socialize" in each other's homes, but organized activities of a class should be controlled from the church. New members can literally be driven away by a status-seeking chairman of social activities who wants the class to spend five dollars a plate for dinner at her country club. These mistakes can be held to a minimum when class functions are held at either the church or a place determined by vote of the entire class.

The difficulties of placing members in homogeneous groups is increased during the upsurge of a revival service when inquirers enter the church without many previous contacts with its membership. The problem is especially acute during community revivals when churches of various social strata participate in one meeting. How will the inquirer make his choice? Such questions call for renewed attention to the pastoral-care aspects of revivalism, which will be considered in the next two chapters.

8

The Pastoral Aspects of Revivalism

Revivalism and pastoral care are both aspects of evangelism.[1] Unfortunately, the two have often been considered contradictory rather than complementary. During the first American revival, the Great Awakening, Gilbert Tennent was accused of pastoral negligence because he spent time preaching outside his own church. Timothy Cutler thrust at the personal damage of Tennent's preaching when he wrote: "[Tennent told his hearers] that they were damned! damned! damned! This charmed them; and, in the most dreadful winter I ever saw, people wallowed in snow, night and day, for the benefit of his beastly brayings; and many ended their days under these fatigues." [2]

After the nation-wide campaigns of Dwight L. Moody, more accurate criticisms were voiced. Upon the urging of Mr. Moody, a Baptist minister, George Pentecost, became a full-time evangelist in 1878. In 1900 he issued this judgment: "The future evangelist will be the associate and helper of the pastor or pastors . . . and not the 'boss of the whole show' . . . the new revival . . . will be carried on by individual churches or small combinations of churches of the same denominations." [3]

This much of Mr. Pentecost's prediction has come to pass in

[1] "Revivalism" may be described as commitment to organized, periodic campaigns by a church or churches for the purpose of evangelizing the community and reviving the churches.

[2] Quoted in E. S. Gaustad, *The Great Awakening in New England* (New York: Harper & Brothers, 1957), p. 152. Actually, Tennent was a good pastor, as will be seen in a later section, "Diligent Personal Care."

[3] Quoted in McLoughlin, *op. cit.*, p. 348.

some churches. Unfortunately, we have not yet realized another of his admonitions. "Conversions . . . should be obtained by patient and serious pastoral consultation and not in 'after meetings' where 'indiscriminate "workers" with a few texts of Scripture' seek to 'railroad inquirers' into hasty and shallow decisions to accept Christ." [4] Baptists like Mr. Pentecost and President Horr of Newton Theological Institute called for "personal evangelism" or "pastoral evangelism." They wanted every pastor to preach like an evangelist and every Christian to win his neighbors to Christ.

By 1922, a "new evangelism" had emerged. This was visitation evangelism, a door-to-door campaign for converts. A. Earl Kernahan developed visitation campaigns throughout the nation. The hastiness of his work may be judged by his estimate that in two hours laymen could be trained to sell Christianity.[5] In the 1950's this became denominational programs such as "New Life" for Presbyterians or "Tidings" for Methodists and others. Mass visitation replaced mass meetings.

Do these developments mean that revivalism and pastoral care are to go their separate ways? No, although *some* revivalists and *some* pastoral counselors will never be together.[6] But revivalists with a pastor's heart and pastors with an evangelistic zeal can work together. In fact, there are at least five pastoral aspects of revivals which condition the spontaneity, duration, and depth of a religious awakening:

(1) Pastoral motivation: revivals often well up from a minister or layman's personal experience of gratitude for the forgiveness of sin, joy in the fellowship of God, and zeal to share this new life with others.

(2) Diligent personal care: by home visitation and office consultation, an enduring evangelist receives the needs of the people as his own and offers his own personality as a channel of Christ's concern for them. In the pulpit the evangelist deals with

---

[4] *Ibid.*

[5] *Ibid.*, p. 460.

[6] For example, "nondirective" counselors who rigidly rule out all "judgments" would be in obvious conflict with evangelists who wish to confront people with the claims of the gospel.

those to whom he has ministered and the people see his preaching translated into personal concern through his visitation.

(3) Responsible fellowship: the church that is disciplined in the gospel and is responsive to human need will refresh those who evangelize, attract those who are unsaved, and conserve those who are converted. The body of Christ, the church, is to the proclaimer of the Word as a prepared field is to the sower of seed.

(4) Fervent preaching: the evangelist articulates his concern for the salvation of all people by preaching that combines personal concern, intimate details about life, theological relevance, and realistic commitment.

(5) New life: the power of the gospel is demonstrated by the personal changes in Christians and the challenges of a revived church to society.

These hypotheses may be demonstrated from the four great seasons of revival in America. William McLoughlin has described these four times of national awakening. The first extended from 1725 to 1750. This was the Great Awakening led by Jonathan Edwards, George Whitefield, Theodore Frelinghuysen, and Gilbert Tennent. The second took place from 1795 to 1835. From the frontiers of Kentucky and upstate New York, men like Charles Finney brought self-reliant individualism into American Protestantism. The pastor became less of a community leader and more of a revivalist. In city and college, Timothy Dwight and Lyman Beecher joined with Finney to substitute "free will" for the predestination of an earlier Calvinism.

The third awakening moved from 1875 to 1915. Dwight L. Moody, Reuben Torrey, and Billy Sunday developed revivalism as a professional organization and renewed the faith of new industrial cities in the old virtues of rural religion. The fourth surge of national interest in religion may be dated from 1945 to at least 1970. The center of attention is Billy Graham, the first Southern Baptist to gain more than regional prominence in revivalism.[7]

[7] This summary is based upon McLoughlin's analysis in *Billy Graham: Revivalist in a Secular Age* (New York: The Ronald Press, 1960), pp. 3–24, and

Each of these seasons of spiritual renewal contains elements of pastoral concern. From the following discussion perhaps further research can be stimulated among those who see the relevance of pastoral care for revivalism.[8]

Pastoral Motivation

The pastoral elements of revivalism flow together like streams of water that cascade into one fountain. Together they are an arching, living whole. Alone, any one of them is a troublesome jet that sprays out of bounds. For example, a vivid religious experience is an essential aspect of pastoral motivation. But if it is presented without sensitivity to the needs of others, it soon becomes a club used to force conformity. The evangelist insists that all must be saved his way. The varieties of conversion are not considered because the revivalist has no personal interest in, or respect for, those whom he would "coerce" into the kingdom of God.

Pastoral motivation should combine personal conviction and group acceptance. Of primary importance is the mediation of the gospel to the minister through a group of consecrated believers. When the evangelist receives Christ through the Christian fellowship which is his body, he is more likely to develop warm relationship with converts and cultivate groups for Christian living. Thus the fruits of the Word are nurtured because the sower has been cultivated in the same ground.

One outstanding example of motivation-in-fellowship is John Wesley. By his own testimony, the three "crises" of Methodism may be traced to small groups of believers.[9] The first was the Holy Club at Oxford. Here he found inspiration and articulation

---

Modern Revivalism, pp. 3–11. In commenting on Baptist participation, Professor Leo Garrett wrote, "If our forefathers were petrified on the rock of hyper-Calvinism, we are greased on the slicky-slide of activism," *Baptists and the Awakenings of Modern History,* p. 6.

[8] Scholars may wish to consult the bibliographies on American revivalism in H. Shelton Smith, Robert T. Handy, and L. A. Loetscher, *American Christianity* (New York: Charles Scribner's Sons, 1960), I, 371–73; Weisberger, *op. cit.;* McLoughlin, *Modern Revivalism.*

[9] A. S. Wood, *The Inextinguishable Blaze* (Grand Rapids: Wm. B. Eerdmans Publishing Co., 1960), p. 162.

as a Christian student. The second crisis was the Savannah society. On his sea voyage to Savannah, Wesley saw the serenity of German Moravians in a storm that sent the English into "a terrible screaming." On his first Sunday in Georgia, Wesley sought out the Moravian leader Spangenberg and received from him the direct question: "Do you know Jesus Christ?" For two years Wesley brooded over the question. At the close of his Georgia journal he wrote: "But what have I learned myself in the meantime? Why, what I the least of all suspected, that I, who went to America to convert others, was never myself converted to God." [10]

The decisive crisis came as Wesley sat among a small group of pietists who gathered in Aldersgate Street to read and pray. As someone read Luther's preface to Romans, Wesley felt his own heart strangely warmed: "I felt I did trust in Christ, Christ alone for salvation; and an assurance was given me that He had taken away *my* sins, even *mine,* and saved *me* from the law of sin and death." [11]

The founder of Methodism found his individual assurance in the midst of a corporate worship experience. The impact of this fellowship is seen in his founding of the Fetter Lane Society in the spirit of the Aldersgate assembly. As a Methodist historian states it, "The starting-point in the growth of Methodist organization was the fundamental Christian need for fellowship." [12] Wesley could not preach with power until he was personally gripped by the grace of Christ; but this experience was mediated to him through individuals and a praying fellowship.

The American awakening was heralded by a similar burst of personal conviction that was kindled by the concern of a group. It is the story of the "Log Cabin" preachers. In the early 1700's Scottish and American Presbyterians had settled into apathy under the dead weight of Calvinistic orthodoxy. Ministers were expected to come from a Scottish university, but graduation fell

[10] *The Journal of the Rev. John Wesley* (London: The Epworth Press, 1938), I, 421–22.
[11] *Ibid.,* pp. 475–76.
[12] Wood, *op. cit.,* p. 166.

so low at Edinburgh that in 1745 there were but three graduates, and none in 1746.[13]

Would churches in the colonies far across the Atlantic wait for this trickle from the homeland? The answer came from an Edinburgh graduate, William Tennent. By 1733, he had settled in the middle colonies as pastor, educated three of his sons for the ministry, and seen them ordained with a fourth pupil, Samuel Blair. These men were characterized by personal convictions of their own religious experience, vigorous evangelistic preaching, and intensive and searching counseling with their people. In 1735, William Tennent erected a log cabin for the training of ministers. Out of it came twenty-one men, many of them strategic for the advance of American Presbyterianism.[14]

The "Log Cabin" men were soon the center of theological controversy. They were leaders in Whitefield's American campaign of 1740. The success of that revival increased their proclamation of "enthusiastic" religion. Gilbert Tennent's sermon on "The Danger of an Unconverted Ministry" stressed individual regeneration as the essential condition of a minister's call by God.[15]

This struck at the "Old Side" ministers, who rejected questions about their "soul exercises" as an invasion of their private spiritual life. They counterattacked with an insistence that all ministerial candidates subscribe "without the least variation or alteration" to the literal words of the Westminster Confession, Catechisms, and Directory.[16] "Private" religion and verbal assent to a set of propositions were their defenses against Tennent's call for a public testimony of religious experience. But their isolation and creedal correctness were no match for the combined resources of Log Cabin ministers: personal religious experience, fellowship among regenerate ministers, fervent preaching, and diligent pastoral calling. These were the elements of

[13] L. J. Trinterud, *The Forming of an American Tradition* (Philadelphia: The Westminster Press, 1949), p. 64.

[14] *Ibid.*

[15] *Ibid.*, pp. 89–90; the sermon is reproduced in Smith, Handy, and Loetscher, *op. cit.*, pp. 322–28.

[16] Trinterud, *ibid.*, p. 66.

"New Light" on the Christian life and the ministry. They became the shaping force of American Presbyterianism and a bulwark of revivalism.

Some of these same characteristics have been seen in later revivalists of national prominence. Dwight L. Moody found Christ when his Sunday school teacher came to his place of business for a heart-to-heart talk. Moody knew that he was wanted in a Christian fellowship. Soon he was leading others into pews that he rented at the church, into Y.M.C.A. discussion groups, into personal discussions about Christ. His restless energy brought him acceptance, encouragement, and financial aid from men like Cyrus McCormick and George Armour.

Moody did not have the element of individual pastoral attention that characterized the Log Cabin men. He was too busy to see any one person more than a few minutes. In one day he might make two hundred calls. But he did have the range of ministerial associations that characterizes one who has been called as part of a fellowship. The conservative Moody could work in England with the liberal Henry Drummond.[17] His personal flexibility was one fruit of warm personal relationships.

By contrast, Billy Sunday raged against ministers who deviated from his preconceptions. He denounced "time serving," "hypocritical," "hireling ministers." [18] Was this hostile isolationism a combination of Sunday's personality and a lack of fellowship in the church and the Chicago Y.M.C.A.? Or was his attitude part of a change in the theological and social climate of a new century? Whatever the answer, the results of Sunday's loneliness were isolated, shallow-rooted converts. A year after his Philadelphia revival, only twelve thousand out of forty-one thousand "trail-hitters" had joined a church, and only five thousand of these for the first time. A local minister estimated that many of these five thousand were no longer in the churches.[19]

---

[17] Fundamentalists like C. I. Scofield condemned Moody for his association with Drummond, W. R. Harper, and John A. Broadus. Cole, *op. cit.*, p. 34.

[18] McLoughlin, *Modern Revivalism, op. cit.*, p. 410.

[19] This and additional evidence is presented in *ibid.*, pp. 429–30. The same disheartening statistics could be compiled for a revival in any church that stressed isolationism. See Powell, *op. cit.*, pp. 2 ff.

The evangelist who drinks from a well of loneliness will spit out bitterness. But those who are nurtured in a concerned community are grateful for all who labor with them for the Lord. Great awakenings do not come because *one* torch is lit. The light of God's love smolders in a hundred hamlets where unknown pastors fight indifference and engulfing darkness. Then, when these have done their patient work, the blaze can race through the land, leaping from one man's labor to the next.

This was the way of the Great Awakening. Theodore Frelinghuysen stirred his Dutch Reformed congregations in the middle colonies; Jonathan Dickinson awakened the churches of the New York Presbytery while William Tennent and his sons evangelized in New Brunswick.[20] Jonathan Edwards saw the results of his preaching spread down the Connecticut River Valley in 1734. When George Whitefield came into these areas in 1740, he reaped the harvest which these men and others had sown.[21] Christian fellowship bore fruit in warm concern for others.

Diligent Personal Care

One of the marks of a deep and sustained awakening is diligent personal care for those who seek salvation and those who have found it. When we look behind the sensational results of national revivals, we find the ground for some of them prepared by careful pastoral visitation and counseling. A. Skevington Wood traced the spiritual renewal of the eighteenth century to evangelistic pastors like William McCulloch, who had cared for a Glasgow congregation for eleven years before George Whitefield joined him to witness an outbreak of religious concern.[22] John Wesley recognized as the chief evangelical of 1761 a small-town clergyman, Samuel Walker. Through twenty years of hard and prayerful work, Walker transformed the dissolute town of Truro into "the most Christian town in England." [23]

[20] See "A Revival by Church Discipline" in Smith, Handy, and Loetscher, *op. cit.,* pp. 316–17.
[21] See Gaustad, *op. cit.,* pp. 16–24. A. S. Wood has traced numerous antecedents of the English Methodist revival in *op. cit.*
[22] Wood, *ibid.,* pp. 119–20.
[23] *Ibid.,* pp. 138–41.

In the American phase of the Great Awakening, Jonathan Edwards built upon the foundation of a sixty-year pastorate by Solomon Stoddard. During that time there had been five "harvests" of religious concern.[24] Edwards studied, prayed, and preached in homes and churches for eight years before "the town seemed to be full of the presence of God."[25]

Theodore Frelinghuysen stirred New Jersey Reformed churches by evangelistic preaching, strict enforcement of discipline, and zealous visitation. His success was so impressed upon Gilbert Tennent, that the latter gave himself to "greater earnestness in ministerial labors."[26] Out of labors such as these came the Great Awakening.

The second national revival began in frontier settlements such as Red River and Cane Ridge, Kentucky. With few ministers among these widely-scattered people, there probably was little pastoral care.[27] Starved for spiritual guidance and cultivation, congregations gorged themselves on camp-meeting fare. A few days or weeks of preaching and fellowship was all they might snatch during a lifetime of drudgery, loneliness, and bestiality.[28] Disease, danger, and death were daily eschatological reminders that the time for decision was short. Is it any wonder that emotional excesses were reported at some meetings?

It was during this second awakening that itinerant evangelism began with Charles Finney. This was a new kind of revivalism. In the first awakening, pastors who preached with zeal in their own churches were then invited to preach in neighboring towns. Men and women who had witnessed the results in one church

[24] Gaustad, ibid., p. 17.

[25] Ibid., p. 18. Edwards did not visit systematically. He preferred to spend most of his time in study. He visited upon request and counseled those who came to his study. In introducing a new edition of Edwards' Religious Affections, Professor John Smith commented: "It seems likely that JE did a great deal more pastoral work than has been thought, as his acquaintance with the experience of many different people, recorded in his Faithful Narrative, shows." (Edwards, op. cit., p. 4.)

[26] Trinterud, op. cit., pp. 54–56.

[27] "Probably" means that someone should examine the church minutes and autobiographies of the period to determine the meaning and extent of pastoral care on the frontier.

[28] "Lifetime" in 1800 might have been twenty years. Only one half of the children born in colonial times lived to be young adults.

spread the word to surrounding congregations. There was an
intimate connection between the evangelist's own pastorate
and his revival witness. This was probably favored by an era of
small towns and villages, when commerce flowed up and down
the Connecticut and other rivers through individual trades-
men.

Finney started his ministry in small villages but within seven
years he was preaching in Boston and other seaboard cities. Urban revivalism soon became an organized effort by churches to
support the preaching of an evangelist brought to the city because of his successful preaching in other places. Under such
conditions, who would be responsible for the personal cultivation
of Christians and non-Christians before the preaching began?
The urban leaders of the nineteenth century, Finney and Moody,
gave brief attention to this need by asking for prayer meetings
and visitation before they arrived.[29]

The most intensive effort to bridge the gap between revival
meetings and personal cultivation has been made by Billy
Graham. Six months to a year before his scheduled appearance,
members of his staff arrive in the city. Committees are set up for
daily and weekly prayer groups and pastors and laymen are
taught evangelistic methods until "they start everybody talking
about religion." [30]

Denominational executives have also developed programs for
pre-revival visitation by church members to unsaved and un-
churched persons in the community.[31]

One phase of personal care precedes a revival. Another phase
begins with the meeting and continues after it. During his
American tour, Whitefield wrote: "So many persons come to me
under convictions, and for advice, that I have scarce time to eat
bread." [32] In the first three months after Gilbert Tennent had

[29] McLoughlin, *Modern Revivalism, op. cit.,* pp. 98, 217 ff.

[30] McLoughlin, *Billy Graham, op. cit.,* pp. 167–68. Since this system has
been in use for years it is time for someone to study its effectiveness in one
or more cities.

[31] E.g., three months of "cultivation visitation" before a revival is recommended by a Baptist director of evangelism, C. E. Autrey.

[32] Gaustad, *op. cit.,* p. 27.

preached in Boston, John Webb of New North Church was visited by a thousand persons seeking spiritual counsel.[33]

Those who were awakened wanted personal help. In the eighteenth century, this was provided by pastoral visitation or group meetings in homes or churches. In the nineteenth century an urban setting and an itinerant evangelist intensified the need for pastoral attention for those who were awakened or who needed to be.

In the third national revival, Moody trained "Christian workers" to meet individual converts in the "inquiry room" after the revival service. In *Glad Tidings* and *Great Joy* he included some of his talks to those workers. They were advised to find out the differences in personality and diagnose the religious problem of each inquirer. Once this had been done, the worker should present some Scripture verses or advice which would apply to the individual's condition.[34] Meetings in inquiry rooms established a pattern for "personal work" that has changed very little in a hundred years.

In a modern urban setting, the Graham organization has attempted to train counselors before a meeting begins. Persons who present themselves for such training are required to attend seven out of nine training classes which are directed by a member of the Graham staff. Instructions for the 1957 New York Crusade included this section:

Determine the *need* of the Inquirer.
(a) Encourage the Inquirer to express himself by asking him questions—don't do all the talking.
    (1) What did you have in mind as you came forward tonight?
    (2) What decision have you made or are you making?
    (3) Have you ever made a decision for Christ before?
    (4) How, in your mind, does a person become a Christian?
(b) Look for the basic need.
    (1) *Note*—the Inquirer may think his need is to get

---

[33] *Ibid.*, pp. 34–35.
[34] Moody, *Great Joy, op. cit.*, pp. 277–87.

> over some habit but the real need may be con-
> version.
>
> (2) Quietly *Pray* for wisdom and guidance. James
>   1:5 and Romans 8:14.
>
> Meet the need with the OPEN BIBLE—point them to
> Christ.

Additional instructions were on Scripture verses to be quoted, organizational details, and advice.[35]

The questions are provocative, but the recommendations suffer the usual restrictions of instant evangelism. The instructions contain no information on the dynamics of interviewing. Counselors must make their own connection between the stated needs of the individual and biblical passages on salvation. Dr. Graham has indicated an interest in pastoral counseling in conversation with Dr. Wayne Oates of the Southern Baptist Theological Seminary. Unfortunately, he has not applied this to the instruction of inquiry-room counselors. Pastoral counselors have shown an interest in evangelistic interviewing. When evangelists invite their assistance, inquiry-room techniques may change. It will be quite a challenge, since counselors in the Billy Graham Louisville campaign often interviewed twenty or thirty inquirers each night.[36]

The need for pastoral attention extends beyond the revival into the homes and churches of those who make decisions. What permanent additions are there to the churches? How are the lives of people changed?

Some answers to these questions were provided by Palmer Bowers, who studied reports of the Louisville Graham campaign and interviewed one hundred persons who signed inquirer's cards. As in other studies of records,[37] Mr. Bowers found that most of the inquirers (66 per cent) were already church

---

[35] This instruction book and others are in the Billy Graham collection, Southern Baptist Theological Seminary Library, Louisville, Ky.

[36] Palmer Bowers, "An Evaluation of the Billy Graham Greater Louisville Evangelistic Crusade" (Master's thesis, Southern Baptist Theological Seminary, Louisville, Ky., 1959), p. 18. See also "What's in Store for the Converts?," *Christianity Today*, July 4, 1960.

[37] See McLoughlin, *Modern Revivalism, op. cit.*, pp. 517–19; *Courier Journal*, January 27, 1958.

members. Eight per cent had joined a church since the crusade and 14 per cent were intending to join.[38]

One of the most dismal findings was that pastors paid little attention to the persons listed on decision cards. Although the campaign organization had spent months in the city and had sent decision cards immediately to pastors, only twenty-two out of one hundred inquirers had had a pastoral visit after the Crusade. Sixteen had been contacted by their Crusade counselor.[39] Perhaps the pastors thought their work was done before the Crusade. Seventy-one of the inquirers said that the pastor had visited in their home at some time previous to the Crusade and thirty-five considered him to be a close personal friend. How is this to be evaluated? Do ministers lack interest in the spiritual development of persons who are already on their church rolls? The difficulty was increased in Louisville by the refusal of the Graham organization to administer a follow-up program which was suggested by the local committee.[40]

There certainly was a need for such interest, because there was little change in the religious habits of those interviewed. Mr. Graham placed great emphasis upon prayer, Bible reading, church attendance, and personal morality. Yet Mr. Bowers found that only four out of twenty inquirers who previously drank intoxicating beverages had stopped. Only eight of the one hundred reported a change in prayer habits. There was a small increase in church attendance. Forty increased their Bible reading.[41]

It appears that some revivalism has become an easy substitute for pastoral care. The attitude of some ministers was revealed by the college professor who conducted a revival in the church of which I was pastor. He said: "In most meetings I visit with the pastor from morning till night. We catch up on all the visits he

---

[38] Bowers, *op. cit.*, p. 35. Elton Trueblood wrote "of course many of the converts came out of the churches. From where else could they come, in a society in which most people claim to be church people already?" *The Yoke of Christ* (New York: Harper & Brothers, 1958), pp. 58–59.

[39] Bowers, *op. cit.*, p. 94.

[40] *Ibid.*

[41] *Ibid.*, pp. 52–58, 66–69.

should have made since the last revival." On the day that I write this paragraph, a pastor said to a faculty member: "We'll need at least eight days for this revival. We're really going to visit a lot of people!" What does he mean? Have the minister and church cultivated these people, or will the pastor use the evangelist to make up for the personal work that he has not done for the past fifty-one weeks?

How does such motivation look beside the careful labors of pastoral evangelists like Samuel Blair? Here was a leader of the "Log Cabin" preachers who talked privately with every convert until he was satisfied that the inquirer understood conversion and could see evidences of personal change.[42] Few modern revivals have *that* kind of "old time religion."

Almost one hundred years ago, a Methodist circuit rider who had been converted at Cane Ridge in 1801 looked back over two generations of ministerial work in Kentucky. He wrote:

I suppose since the day of Pentecost, there was hardly ever a greater revival of religion than at Cane Ridge; and if there had been steady, Christian ministers, settled in Gospel doctrine and Church discipline, thousands might have been saved to the Church that wandered off in the mazes of vain, speculative divinity, and finally made shipwreck of the faith, fell back, and turned infidel, and lost their religion and their souls forever.[43]

Responsible Fellowship

Where are the converts? Since the days of Whitefield, this has been the question raised the morning after the meeting of the night before. "The evangelists uniformly blamed this (loss) on the local pastors for not following up and consolidating the conversions made at the meetings. The local ministers complained that the evangelist's converts were only superficially aroused." [44]

Responsibility for care of the converts should be shared by revivalist, pastor, and congregation. The people of the church

---

[42] See Trinterud, *op. cit.*, pp. 78–90.
[43] Peter Cartwright, *Autobiography* (Nashville: Abingdon Press, 1956), p. 33.
[44] McLoughlin, *Billy Graham, op. cit.*, p. 63.

are the ones who can demonstrate a consistent concern for those who would be received into their fellowship. The ground of human relations must be prepared to nurture those who receive the Word. The difficulties of developing this fellowship in revivalism may be seen in the following study. It is a summary of personal interviews with forty-one persons who had joined a "First Church" during a revival. These people were seen one year after their decision to determine the impact of the revival upon their spiritual growth. A member of their family and a friend were also interviewed.

One hundred and twenty-five persons made some kind of decision during the five weeks of the revival. To provide fellowship for these people would require activity in almost every department of the church. Consider the age range of decisions: Adults, 35; Young People, 3; Intermediates, 11; Juniors, 42; Primary, 3.

Over one third of the persons in each age category were interviewed. Fourteen people refused to see an interviewer. The forty-one interviewed came into the church as follows:

	Adult	Young People	Intermediate	Junior
Profession of faith	3	1	8	15 [45]
Transfer of church membership	6			
Statement of previous membership in another church [46]	5			

The variety of decisions creates new challenges for fellowship. The Junior boys need instruction in faith and church membership. Most of them could describe the feeling but not the meaning or content of the decision they had made. The adults need additional help in the transfer from one denomination to an-

---

[45] Twelve boys and three girls!

[46] These might be persons who were inactive members of another church of the same denomination, active or inactive members of churches of other denominations. This was a Southern Baptist church of the majority type which requires baptism of persons coming from other communions.

other and from rural church to urban church. For example, when one woman from the mountains was asked about the beliefs of her former church, she replied, "There are a lot of things we *don't* believe."

The evangelists who conducted this meeting reported that most of the people came from small farming communities to the middle- and lower middle-class section of the city in which this church is located. Who would provide "folksiness" in the midst of a strange new environment?

The need for *some* kind of personal relationship came out of a routine question asked by each interviewer: "Do you have any objection if I talk to some of your family and/or friends about this?"

Many persons had to think for some time before they could suggest the name of a friend in the church or any friend who might give an evaluation of their profession of faith and change of life. Several of the Junior-age boys said that they never talked about religion with their friends. Others found their only religious fellowship in the Sunday school class or in the home of a godly neighbor. One adult expressed his need this way:

I joined a church here when I was fourteen but when I came back from service I never saw any of them unless they wanted money. . . . I just never did get started back. They didn't seem to care if I went. That's one thing I can say for ———— (*the minister of the church he has just joined*) and this church—they visit. . . .
I don't understand some people who claim to be Christians, though. Some of them will speak at church but if they meet you on the street or any place away from the church they act like they don't even know you.

This man confessed that he had little confidence in himself. He joined the church because he admired the pastor who "made me feel like he wanted me to come to church, to be a part of it." His wife said that the pastor was influential. She had also been concerned about her husband's church attendance and had offered to attend any church with him. She and the son joined the church some time before the husband did.

When the revival meeting ended, the church left little impression of fellowship upon the converts. When asked, "What has happened since your decision?" the interviewees gave no examples of visitation from church members or closer fellowship in church meetings. The closest sentiment to this was one comment: "Well, you have to be a member to let the people know you want to be one of them." Several persons mentioned a closer fellowship in their own family but there was little reference to the new family of God which they had joined.

To most of the converts the pastor was the major influence upon their decision. Within three months after the revival the pastor moved to another church. By this time some of the converts were already inactive. Seven months later, one man did not know that the pastor was gone. Others said, "Well, I went some, but when Brother ——— left, I just quit."

The indifference of the church and the family seemed to be more detrimental than the pastor's resignation. When families and neighbors supported each other in Christian attitudes, prayer, and church attendance, membership was consistent. But for others, family support was weak and neighbors were not mentioned. A convert who remained active observed that a few people did most of the work in the church. They were already overburdened. Who would care for new people?

What happens when pastor, evangelist, and church members decrease their obvious interest in converts when the revival is over? To find some answers, one year later the persons who joined First Church during the revival were divided into four groups:

> Nuclear members: those who are regular in their church attendance and assume some responsibility as a member of a church committee, an officer, or a teacher. 6%

> Modal members: those who consider themselves to be members in good standing, attend fairly often or regularly the Sunday school and/or Sunday morning worship service. 42%

Marginal members: those who consider
themselves to be members of the church but
almost never attend any of its services.   50%

Dormant members: those who are voted into
the church after they walk down the aisle
but do not return to the church.   2% [47]

Since children are not asked to assume teaching or committee
responsibilities, there were no "nuclear" members below the
age of sixteen. The percentage of marginal and modal members
was similar in all age groups.

Looking back, a church leader commented that they had not
really prepared for new members. Space was inadequate for
Sunday school classes. New teachers and visitors had not been
trained. Imagine the impact of 125 new additions to a church
of under five hundred members! "We just couldn't handle those
who crowded in, and soon they were gone," he said. One positive result of the revival was a decision to build additional educational space.

Is this study representative of revivals? When more studies
have been made, we can more adequately answer that question.[48]
In the meantime, some denominations show hopeful signs of
concern for an enduring fellowship. Denominational instructions
on pre-revival visitation by laymen do increase personal contacts. If this could be followed up by similar visits after the meeting, gains could be consolidated into growing lives. An example of this later emphasis is a new program of visitation by deacons in Southern Baptist churches.

The problem of a vital church affiliation is also perennial with
converts from national revivals. In the testimonials solicited by
Robert Ferm there are several references to this problem. Inquirers from the Graham crusades sometimes went from one
church to another until they found one that gave "a clear

[47] A similar classification for Catholic parishioners may be found in Joseph H. Fichter, *Social Relations in the Urban Parish* (Chicago: University of
Chicago Press, 1954).

[48] A more detailed study of the data used in this section is being made by
L. O. Mills as part of his Th.D. dissertation, Southern Baptist Theological
Seminary, Louisville, Ky.

presentation of the gospel." [49] One girl moved to a chapel where there was "lots of Bible study" after her minister made slurring remarks about Graham.[50] A young man faced the embarrassment of confessing, "As a Sunday school teacher and church worker, I hadn't even been a Christian." [51] Some converts affiliated with no church but seemed to find fellowship in Bible study groups in school or the home of another convert.[52]

National revivalists also face the need to perpetuate their evangelistic emphasis. The answer has usually been to found a college or seminary for the training of ministers and lay evangelists. This fellowship-for-evangelism has produced Tennent's "Log Cabin," Finney's Oberlin College, and Moody's Bible Institute. A later phase of their ministries was given to the building up of these institutions.[53] Only Billy Sunday remained isolated until the end. And it was after his hostilities that revivalism went into almost total eclipse among the major Protestant denominations. Bishop Joseph Berry, who sponsored Billy Sunday in 1912, four years later issued the following criticisms of present-day evangelism: (1) the "two weeks of vitriolic attack upon ministers and church members"; (2) exaltation of the revivalist and lack of recognition for supporting ministers; (3) the "superficial and perilous" method of dealing with inquirers by nothing more than a shake of the hand; (4) the overemphasis upon statistics; (5) "vulgar display" of gifts presented to the revivalist; (6) high pressure methods to obtain freewill offerings.[54]

Revivalism has been revived itself because men like Billy Graham have taken constructive measures to avoid many of these criticisms. The major modern criticism is the instability of

[49] *Persuaded to Live* (Westwood, N. J.: Fleming H. Revell Co., 1958), pp. 93, 182.

[50] *Ibid.*, pp. 131–32.

[51] *Ibid.*, p. 105.

[52] *Ibid.*, pp. 93, 153.

[53] What will Graham do? By identification with the Southern Baptist Convention, he has not felt the need to develop an interdenominational seminary, as Moody and Finney did. Will his organizational activities flow through denominational channels or will his time, like Moody's, be increasingly consumed in the maintenance of new, independent institutions?

[54] McLoughlin, *Modern Revivalism*, p. 447.

converts. Is this an inevitable weakness of national revivals or is
it a problem of all evangelistic efforts—local and national? Can
revivalists perfect an emphasis and organization that will incor-
porate converts into the body of Christ as part of a local church?
Can pastors and laymen revive their churches so that converts
will be attracted to rather than repelled from them?

Fervent Preaching

Part of the answer to these questions will be found in the public statements of revivalists. From the platform they shape the
image, project the expectations of a new life in Christ. There are
at least four elements in revival messages that develop the pastoral aspects of evangelism. They are: (1) the revivalist's personal concern for those who hear him; (2) his portrayal of intimate details from his life and the lives of others; (3) the
theological relevance of the message to daily living; (4) a call to
realistic commitment. These will be illustrated from the sermons
of Billy Graham which were reprinted in the *Nashville Banner*
during his August 22 to September 19, 1954, crusade in that
city.[55]

The personal manner and the sermon content of Graham's
messages demonstrate his concern for those who hear him. In
humility he credits individuals in the audiences for the success
of his meetings: "You know why God blessed the meetings in
London. It wasn't great organization. It certainly wasn't great
preaching. It was because millions of people around the world
banded themselves to pray. I was lifted up night after night on
the power of prayer." [56]

Such comments make each hearer a person of importance. His
prayer and the prayers of others like him empower this campaign. In another sermon, Graham praised those who brought
their Bibles.[57] They could give witness to their concern by com-

---

[55] These sermon reprints and tape recordings of others are available in the
Billy Graham Research Room, Southern Baptist Theological Seminary Library,
Louisville, Ky.

[56] "Reprint of Sermon Texts from the Billy Graham Crusade in Nashville,
August 22 to September 19" (*Nashville Banner*, 1954, p. 6).

[57] *Ibid.*, p. 7.

ing with their Bibles. They could participate in the service by silently following the Scripture passages he read, and find there an authentication for questions or statements made by the revivalist. Critics of Graham have said nothing to cast doubt upon the sincerity of his attempts to identify the prayer and practice of his supporters as the strength of his work. After having sat with disgust through meetings in which other revivalists mouthed phrases like "my humble ministry," I can testify to the delight of hearing Graham preach with humility and sincerity.

Personal concern is most vividly portrayed in Graham's identification with the feelings of his audience. This arrests their attention, melts their defenses, and causes some to feel that he "really understands." Here is a paragraph from the first third of a revival sermon: "Now it is pretty difficult to admit that you are a sinner. That's a bitter pill to swallow, to just stand up and say 'I am a sinner.' That's humiliating. . . . But the Bible says we have broken the law of God and to break the law means that you are a sinner." [58]

A second pastoral element is the inclusion of intimate details about life. The audience readily identifies with the humanity of a speaker like Graham when he illustrates consecration: "Eleven years ago my wife took my name. Her name is Ruth Graham now, not Ruth Bell." He then describes how she would uphold his name if other women criticized him at some social gathering. In the same way Christians are to stand for Christ wherever they are, for they now bear his name.[59] How simple it is for each man and woman to identify with this illustration, to put his or her name in the place of "Graham."

The revivalist also gives conversational details from his encounters with both famous and unknown persons. He reported a general's description of a dissolute life which was finally reclaimed. This was in the final section of a message on "transformation." [60] With these intimate details the evangelist offers proof that a "man's man" can be changed.

[58] *Ibid.*
[59] *Ibid.*, p. 8.
[60] *Ibid.*, p. 4.

A third element is the theological relevance of the message for daily life. The method of Graham is as good at this point as at the first two. He structures theological problems in personal dialogue. Popular assumptions such as "it's enough if you're sincere" are adroitly demolished with popular examples of their absurdity. In one sermon Graham told of a Rose Bowl game in which he saw a player run forty-five yards to the wrong goal line. He was sincere, but he had the wrong goal.[61]

The theological relevance of Graham's sermons is limited by insufficient knowledge of personality dynamics. The revivalist emphasizes present decisions and gives little attention to future developmental problems. It is assumed that after a commitment is made, an act of the will keeps it inviolate.[62] After hearing Graham, during the Louisville campaign, Wayne Oates commented: "Graham has yet to think through his conception of personality and square it with the biblical view of the wholeness of man." Also, Graham offers little more than reassurance for the chronically insecure. He does not consider the pathological factors in religious experience. Four practices are continually presented as necessary for spiritual maturity: Bible reading, daily prayer, church attendance, and personal witnessing for Christ. These can become mere rituals, or even threadbare compulsions, when they are used by emotionally sick people.[63]

Despite these very real limitations, Graham can be specific enough for people to know that religion can be relevant. For example, in a denunciation of the sin of pride, Graham attacked the complacency of those who say "We're a city of churches . . . we don't have the crime rate that New Orleans has. We're not as wicked as Chicago." [64] Yet the audience is corrupt:

The Scripture says, "Thou shalt not kill." You say, "Well, Billy, I've never killed a person." There's more than one way to kill a person.

[61] *Ibid.*, p. 5.

[62] In the inquiry rooms, a member of the Graham staff lays the same emphasis upon an act of the will and the intellectual claims of the gospel. See Bowers, *op. cit.*, p. 16.

[63] Simon Doniger (ed.), *Evangelism and Pastoral Psychology* (Great Neck, N. Y.: Pastoral Psychology Press, 1956), pp. 29–30.

[64] *Nashville Banner*, p. 5.

You can take a gun and shoot them, you can stab them in the back with a knife, but there's many a husband who has sent his wife to an early grave by the way he's treated her, and God Almighty is going to hold you guilty of murder.[65]

Further, Graham lays the same sin upon young people who are sending parents to an early grave, laborers who loaf, employers who squeeze the last ounce of effort from workers, and children who cheat in school.[66] Even "pillars of the church" are not immune. Those who boast of their "Christian experience" are sinners.

National pride is deceitful. A better standard of living does not buy friendship from the peoples of the world. Furthermore, "we have become proud as a race. . . . Three-fifths of the world is not white. . . . We have been proud and thought we were better than any other race, any other people. Ladies and gentlemen, we are going to stumble into hell because of our pride." [67]

The revival climax is an appeal for realistic commitment. This is the fourth element to be considered from a pastoral point of view. It is the weakest. Graham's appeal is to an instantaneous act of the will. Everything is promised to the hearer who will make a decision: "In a moment you can say yes to Christ and leave here tonight having every sin you've ever committed forgiven." [68] As Kurt and Gladys Lang observed in their analysis of Graham's sermons in the 1957 New York Crusade, the decision is supposed to be hard, but is really very easy.[69]

In the closing moments of one message Graham gave this assurance:

When you repent, it means that you confess it, that you're sorry for it, but more, it means that you turn from it. God forgave David his

[65] *Ibid.*, p. 6.
[66] *Ibid.*
[67] *Ibid.*
[68] *Ibid.*, pp. 3–4.
[69] "Decisions for Christ: Billy Graham in New York," Maurice Stein and Others, *Identity and Anxiety* (New York: Free Press of Glencoe, Inc., 1960), pp. 424–27. The authors present their righteous indignation in sociological language.

sin because David never committed it again. David truly repented—
he never went back to that sin. Tonight I'm asking you to make a
resolve in your heart that you're going to turn from sin, that you're
going to live a different life from this moment on. . . .[70]

How does this commitment take place? For only a few is it
the instantaneous and impregnable resolve that Graham presents. The majority of converts change slowly and hesitatingly,
and for some the difference is imperceptible. Commitment to
Christ may be encouraged by a public decision in a mass meeting, but there also must be announcement of the arduous and
lifelong task of consecration that will follow this decision. This
is the problem of individual and social change in conversion
which will be investigated in the following chapter.[71]

[70] *Nashville Banner*, p. 8.
[71] These four criteria for revival preaching suffer from at least one outstanding weakness. They measure *my* evaluation of pastoral elements in a sermon.
A more reliable study would be based on a content analysis of all the sermons
in a crusade and interviews with all the converts. From them we could find
something of the personal impact of Graham's message.

9

Individual and Social Change

The application of Christian resources to personal motivation is another pastoral aspect of revivalism. The power of the gospel is proclaimed through its impact upon individuals and social institutions. The two cannot be separated. Social changes influence revivals and revivals are followed by social reform.[1] Individuals are saved through the mediation of a fellowship and the fellowship is revived through the personal commitment of individuals.

The interrelationship of personal and community forces in revivals may be demonstrated from McLoughlin's *Modern Revivalism* and Timothy Smith's *Revivalism and Social Reform.*

McLoughlin looks to a "particular combination of men and events" for the production of national evangelistic movements. Four general circumstances are present: a major theological reorientation which is connected to a larger intellectual ferment in society; a resultant ecclesiastical conflict in which personalities play a large part; awareness of a social and spiritual cleavage within the churches and between church and world; feeling by those outside the churches that the Christian message is relevant to their contemporary situation.[2] The book weaves these circumstances into a framework that includes extensive reference

[1] The processes of social change have been described in R. M. MacIver, *Society* (New York: The Macmillan Co., 1938); N. L. R. Sims, *The Problem of Social Change* (New York: Thomas Y. Crowell Co., 1939); W. F. Ogburn, *Social Change with Respect to Culture and Original Nature* (New York: Huebsch, B. W., 1922); Talcott Parsons, *The Structure of Social Action* (New York: Free Press of Glencoe, 1948). The application of these sources to revivalism might indicate the institutionalization of revivals. That which was a spontaneous outbreak on the frontier has become a yearly sacrament in staid churches.

[2] *Modern Revivalism, op. cit.,* p. 7.

to individual revivalists, such as Finney, Moody, Sunday, and Graham.

Smith presents the challenging thesis that in mid-nineteenth-century America, the quest for personal holiness drove Christians toward social reform. "Far from disdaining earthly affairs, the evangelists played a key role in the widespread attack upon slavery, poverty, and greed. They thus helped prepare the way both in theory and in practice for what later became known as the social gospel." [3] This thesis is consistent with the social impact of pre-Civil War pietism which has been traced by Alice F. Tyler in *Freedom's Ferment: Phases of American Social History to 1860*.

Personal Transformation

The ingredients of social change are precipitated into a revival when personal transformations occur. In the English Awakening of the 1740's, the herald of evangelicalism was Samuel Walker. Within a few years after he began to preach in Truro, a dissolute soldier was converted. His subsequent constancy of life under provocation was very encouraging to his pastor. When the soldier died, so many persons began to inquire after salvation that Walker had to rent two rooms for the purpose of counseling. [4]

In America, Jonathan Edwards observed an increase in "the tempo of religious activity" after a young woman of questionable morality was converted. As more sought after salvation, eyewitness reports of personal changes spread the news, and the revival, to the neighboring towns. [5]

Over two hundred years later, Billy Graham's Los Angeles Campaign of 1949 caught national attention when J. Arthur Vaus, an associate of Mickey Cohen, professed religion and confessed to the Los Angeles police that he had recently given perjured testimony. [6]

Personal attention to the lives of converts led Jonathan Ed-

---

[3] *Revivalism and Social Reform* (New York: Abingdon Press, 1957), p. 8.
[4] Wood, *op. cit.*, p. 140.
[5] Gaustad, *op. cit.*, pp. 18–19.
[6] McLoughlin, *Billy Graham, op. cit.*, pp. 49–50.

wards to write his *Narrative* and *Treatise Concerning Religious Affections*. The transformation of "sick souls" was an absorbing interest of the psychologist William James. A major portion of his *Varieties of Religious Experience* concerns the personality changes that condition and result from conversion. Begbie documented these changes, as he interpreted James, in *Twice-Born Men*. Robert Ferm in *Persuaded to Live* has presented testimonies from inquiries at Graham campaigns. From these and other works it is evident that individual regeneration is the primary evidence of a true revival.

How stable is the evidence? Are there demonstrable changes in the lives of converts? What are the signs of a more abundant life? In what way may the profession be demonstrated in family, work, and society for years to come? These questions are a perennial embarrassment to revivalists. In the latter days of his ministry, Moody more and more spoke in churches so that the church members might be "quickened" as individual soul-winners. Thus the revival might be more lasting and far-reaching.[7] Edwards admitted that by the time his *Narrative* was published, the surge of interest in Northampton had declined. When Whitefield preached in Edward's church, he wrote "tho' their former Fire might be greatly abated, yet it immediately appeared, when stirred up." [8]

What are the evidences of personal transformation today?

Dr. Pitirim Sorokin, Harvard sociologist, interviewed or received questionnaires from seventy-three converts from revivals of Billy Graham or Bryan Green. He concluded that only one of the seventy-three had shown a tangible change of personality and overt behavior. About half of the converts "talked more like fundamentalists" after the experience, but there was no perceptible change in their outward conduct.[9] Similarly, the investigations of converts in the Louisville Graham crusade, referred to

[7] McLoughlin, *Modern Revivalism, op. cit.,* p. 271.
[8] Gaustad, *op. cit.,* p. 28.
[9] Abraham Maslow (ed.), *New Knowledge in Human Values* (New York: Harper & Brothers, 1959), pp. 4–5. Unfortunately, the conclusions cannot be checked because Dr. Sorokin's interview forms are no longer available. The study was made in 1951.

in chapter eight, gave little evidence of change in the area of religious or irreligious practices.

In contrast, Robert Ferm presents successful conversion stories from other Billy Graham crusades. His is a popular account which contains no mention of failure either in the present constancy of the converts or in the lives of others who made decisions during the crusades. The material seems to be based upon testimonials solicited by the Graham organization. No opinions from character witnesses or interviewers are included. Since the book is not a research study, its chief value is the personal account of changes experienced by some inquirers.

It is easier to answer questions about personal change in a local congregation than in a national campaign. Converts can be personally interviewed. Members of the family, friends, and church workers can be contacted for their evaluations. This was done in the "First Church" study. One question asked of the convert was: "What has happened since your decision in yourself, your family, your work?" More than half (thirty out of forty-one) thought there had been some changes after the revival experience. Most of these were differences in attitudes. When relatives or friends were asked about these thirty converts, a majority confirmed this opinion. For the rest of the converts, family and friends could see no difference in the person before or after the revival.

Only in a few instances could definite transformations be described. These were usually in relationships with others or new concepts of self.[10] For example, a husband and wife who professed faith in Christ during the revival described their home as "happier." The husband stopped drinking. His church attendance is still irregular. The wife enjoyed hearing the children's prayers after she made her decision. A neighbor commented that she had not seen much wrong with the wife before she joined the church. Now she observes that the wife talks a little more about religion. In another family a husband who joined stated that he "felt closer" to his wife since they both were con-

[10] The fulfilment of selfhood through Christian conversion is a major theme of Wayne Oates in *Christ and Selfhood* (New York: Association Press, 1961).

verted. The wife stated that she had meaning and security in life since the decision. Death did not terrify her as it formerly had.

An adolescent boy said that he was more willing to help around the house than he had been before a profession of faith. His mother told the interviewer that her son was now more concerned for "the home and family," especially when there was any illness. The boy commented that he felt his prayers had helped in his mother's recent recovery from an illness. A neighbor saw no change in the boy.

A Junior boy answered the question about change by saying that he felt some guilt about his treatment of a younger brother. When his mother was interviewed, she said: "He hasn't been living like he should. I know it's partly my fault. I've been too lazy to get him up and dressed on Sunday morning, and I don't go with him."

Sometimes the changes were inward. An adolescent girl said that she made a profession to "be closer to Christ." She was a shy person who appreciated the attention of the pastor before the revival. She lived with foster parents with whom she seemed to have a good relationship. Yet she appeared to lack direction or approval for her life. The decision gave her identity with the best authorities in the church and security with God. Her foster mother observed no change in her except a willingness to get up and dress for church on Sunday.

Many methodological problems appear from this kind of investigation. First, the assessment of personality change is complex. Second, the subject is elusive. Who can adequately describe his experience with God and the church? Third, the converts were in the artisan and skilled-labor social class; they were not trained to articulate deeper feelings, although most of those who saw a change would refer to it as a change of feeling. Fourth, the interviewers were dependent upon verbal reports; they did not have opportunity to see the converts before, during, or after the revival service.

The study produced some impressions which have theological implications. One is that converts were seeking something for themselves rather than giving themselves to someone or something. Momentary self-interest and enthusiasm were seen rather than commitment and joy in service. Second, interviewers sensed a nonchalant, casual matter-of-factness in many descriptions of the decision and the present state of converts. Only in a few instances was there awesome reverence and evidence of continuing spiritual struggle.

Although the preaching of the revivalist and the practice of the pastor stressed the "plan of salvation," interviewers found in the converts little sense of divine wrath, agony of conscience, humiliation before God, and joy in deliverance. These are the classical elements of the conversion experience. Why are they not here?

It is tempting to speculate upon all the implications of these preliminary findings. Yet it is better to call for more careful investigation which would include knowledge of the converts before their decision; analysis of the revival sermons and their impact upon the hearers; awareness of the influence which family and church have upon converts before, during, and after their decision; observation of the pastor and revivalist's personal work with converts; testimony from converts and other witnesses of their life after the decision.

In the meantime, revivalists may ponder the gulf between pulpit promises of instantaneous change and the observable lack of transformation in many of these revival converts.

Social Reform

The ferment of personal transformation yields social reformation. New citizens of the kingdom of God act as leaven in society. If power from God is in them, their surroundings will be changed, even as yeast turns meal into dough (Matt. 13:33). The social implications of revivalism were progressive in three of our four national awakenings. The revivals of 1740 and 1820 were characterized by community change and political action. Edwards reported changes in the entire town. Frontiersmen testified that order came out of chaos and decency replaced drunken bullying. The first American Protestant missionaries to the Indians were inspired by the Great Awakening. The crusade for temperance, emancipation of slaves, and social welfare work came out of the holiness preaching of pre-Civil War revivals.[11] The major opponents of revivalists were the social conservatives of established churches.[12]

After the Civil War, America and its evangelism changed. The war hastened the rush of industrialism and urbanization. The open hearth and the Bessemer furnace ushered in the age of iron and steel. The ever-increasing needs of new industry for cheap labor drew five million immigrants to America in the 1880's, nine million in the 1900's. The population increased from four million in 1790 to forty million in 1870. Jobs in commerce and industry attracted immigrant and native farmers to the city. From 1860 to 1890, the urban population increased from 16 to 30 per cent of the total American census. In the North, urbanization followed quickly upon industrialization.

Then came secularization.[13] The aftermath of the Civil War was an accentuation of materialism and public corruption. This was the "Gilded Age." [14] Between 1868 and 1871, the Tweed Ring took between fifty and two hundred million dollars from the public treasury of New York City.[15] The scandals of the Grant administration revealed the ethical failure of the churches.

[11] See Timothy Smith, *op. cit.*, pp. 159, 170, 180, 215. McLoughlin accuses Finney of refusing to follow the social implications of his preaching (pp. 101, 107), but admits his strong stand against slavery (108 ff.). McLoughlin's accusations are further weakened by Finney's interest in benevolent enterprises recorded in Smith, *op. cit.*, pp. 60 ff.

[12] Timothy Smith, *ibid.*, p. 85. In his chapters on "Moral Reformation" and "Perfect Sanctification," Whitney Cross in *The Burned-over District* (Ithaca: Cornell University Press, 1950), describes the campaigns against slavery, intemperance, vice, and for personal piety after Finney's upstate New York campaigns.

[13] Estimates of religious change in this period are given by Cole, *op. cit.*, chap. 2; Shailer Mathews, *The Church and the Changing Order* (New York: The Macmillan Co., 1907); G. B. Smith, *Social Idealism and the Changing Theology: a Study of the Ethical Aspects of Christian Doctrine* (New York: The Macmillan Co., 1913); William Lawrence, *Fifty Years* (New York: Houghton Mifflin, 1923); and W. J. Tucker, *My Generation: An Autobiographical Interpretation* (New York: Houghton Mifflin Co., 1919).

[14] See Charles A. Beard, *The Rise of American Civilization* (New York: The Macmillan Co., 1927), pp. 383 ff.

[15] W. E. Garrison, *The March of Faith* (New York: Harper & Brothers, 1933), p. 61.

Some of the culpable public officials were prominent church people.[16]

Northern churches showed no alarm, for they were at the "summit of complacency." [17] In their eyes the moral righteousness of their cause had been vindicated by the military defeat of slaveholders. The movement of people to cities filled the existing churches. Wealthy industrialists built finer sanctuaries. Who would raise the specter of church discipline against a socially prominent layman who happened to dip heavily into the public treasury? Why should anyone be doubtful when the Methodists were building two churches a week and Henry Ward Beecher was preaching to a packed Brooklyn congregation for $10,000 a year?

Beneath this crust of complacency the foundations were shifting. From 1860 to 1870, church membership dropped from 22.7 per cent of the population to 17.5 per cent. By 1880 it was just up to 20.4 per cent.[18] The "Great Barbecue" of postwar years broke up under the impact of the 1873 depression and convulsive labor strikes in 1877, 1886, and 1892. By the 1890's, some churchmen were beginning to ask some serious questions. Why had it happened?

Looking back upon the post-Civil War period, Francis Weisenburger lists the following reasons why "some church pews were empty": many people felt they could not attain the moral and spiritual requirements of an earlier generation; acrimonious debate between northern and southern churchmen; hypocrisy of church people as religion and ethics were separated; lack of vitality in worship services; religious bickering and narrow denominationalism; decline of rural areas; impersonal and class-conscious atmosphere of urban life; adjustment for immigrants; strict sabbath observance and temperance; indifference in the wake of an increasing secularism.[19]

[16] Henry F. May, *Protestant Churches and Industrial America* (New York: Harper & Brothers, 1949), p. 54.

[17] *Ibid.*, chap. 2.

[18] Latourette, *The Nineteenth Century Outside Europe* (New York: Harper & Brothers, 1961), p. 81.

[19] Francis Weisenburger, *Ordeal of Faith* (New York: Philosophical Library, 1959), pp. 35–40. Other analyses of this period may be found in Aaron Abell,

These currents of history affected much more than church attendance. They challenged the folkways of ante bellum, agrarian religion. How would the individualistic ideals of frontier revivalism relate to a society that was one-sixth urban in 1860 and one-third urban in 1890? What would churchmen say to new ways of thought: pragmatism, biblical criticism, social evolution? [20]

Two vigorous answers appeared. Both stressed personal regeneration. One was the social gospel. The Baptist theologian Walter Rauschenbusch taught that conversion was a personal crisis in a sinful life when a man was brought to accept Christ as Saviour. But it also may be a break with the sinful past of his social group. Deep religious experiences are social as well as individual.

It has always been recognized that the creation of regenerate personalities, pledged to righteousness, is one of the most important services which the Church can render to social progress. But regeneration merely creates the will to do the right; it does not define for a man what is right. That is defined for him in the main by the religious community whose ideas he accepts.[21]

The unrest of the late nineteenth century in northern America centered about labor relations. Exponents of the social gospel spoke and acted on economic and political issues of labor and management.[22] The ideal of these churchmen was a regenerate man in a redeemed society.

Yet the social gospel gradually drew away from evangelical

The Urban Impact on American Protestantism (Cambridge: Harvard University Press, 1943); May, *op. cit.;* C. H. Hopkins, *The Rise of the Social Gospel in American Protestantism, 1865–1915* (New Haven: Yale University Press, 1940); and Latourette, *The Nineteenth Century Outside Europe, op. cit.* Latourette has a tone of optimism in his discussion of increased church membership. Yet, he cautions: "To what extent the numerical increase indicated an augmentation of Christian character in the population as a whole would be impossible to determine" (p. 82).

[20] Many of these issues are discussed by Weisenburger, *ibid.*, chaps. 4–13.

[21] Walter Rauschenbusch, *Christianity and the Social Crisis* (New York: The Macmillan Co., 1907), p. 354. See also Rauschenbusch, *A Gospel for the Social Awakening* (New York: Association Press, 1950), pp. 103–7.

[22] See Hopkins, *op. cit.*

conversion, for it was anteceded by Horace Bushnell's *Christian Nurture*. Charles Hopkins traced the origins of social Christianity to Bushnell, who broke down the extreme individualism of the old Puritanism.[23] From him came a reliance on social processes and decreasing emphasis upon the individual crisis of decision for salvation.[24]

By the turn of the century the movement was turning from the biblically-inspired ideal of the kingdom of God toward a humanistic emphasis on the Jesus of history. In contrast to Rauschenbusch, Shailer Mathews of the University of Chicago taught that religious presuppositions were incidental to Christian social enterprises.[25] By 1913, the Northern Baptist Theological Seminary was established as an evangelical protest against the "process theology" of Chicago's divinity school. A few years before, a University of Chicago professor, George Foster, was disfellowshipped from the Chicago Baptist Ministers' Conference for repudiating the "Bible plan of salvation" in his book *The Finality of the Christian Religion*.[26]

The other answer to nineteenth-century problems was personal regeneration which was undergirded by traditional social assumptions. This was the powerful thrust of the third national revival. Moody rejected the social gospel doctrine of the fatherhood of God and the brotherhood of man. His answer to community issues was: "A heart that is right with God and man seldom constitutes a social problem and by seeking first the kingdom of God and his righteousness nine tenths of social betterment is effected by the convert himself and the other tenth by Christian sympathy." [27]

In the following decade, this sentiment hardened into revival support for reactionary politicians. Sam Jones excoriated the liberal mayor of Toledo and Billy Sunday held a "Salvation

---

[23] *Ibid.*, p. 5, and Arthur McGiffert, *The Rise of Modern Religious Ideas* (New York: The Macmillan Co., 1915), p. 277.
[24] The influence of evolutionary process upon the social gospel is traced by Hopkins, *op. cit.*, pp. 123–29.
[25] *Ibid.*, pp. 204 ff.
[26] Cole, *op. cit.*, p. 90.
[27] Quoted in McLoughlin, *Modern Revivalism*, p. 277.

Circus" in Colorado following a pitched battle between strikers and National Guardsmen.[28] In each instance the revivalists seemed to have been the unwitting tools of unscrupulous individuals. They were betrayed by their naïve rejection of the social impact of the gospel and a trust in superficial slogans for society.

The heritage of the third national awakening was a curious reversal of earlier revivals. There was no harvest of new benevolent enterprises which was the "ferment of freedom" in 1740 and 1825. Instead, there was a widening gap between revivalistic proponents of post-Civil War "old time religion" and liberal exponents of the "social gospel."

The pastoral consequences of this split were devastating. Seekers were now presented with a choice between individual redemption and the reconstruction of their community. In late nineteenth-century revivalism, the "soul" was extracted from the body. The biblical emphasis upon interpersonal relations was neglected; and a Greek theory of a disembodied, immortal soul was used to justify this narrow concept of salvation.[29] A mountain preacher reared under such teaching describes its influence:

I discovered as I studied my Bible that the Gospel of Jesus meant more than saving souls from the standpoint that I conceived of a "soul." (In my background) the "soul" is a little thing inside of you and it's distinct and it's extracted and it goes to heaven and the rest goes to the devil if he wants it. I got a different view from studying the Bible—God was trying to save *people*. He wanted to save the whole man.[30]

On the other hand, the social gospel movement left the evangelical emphasis of Rauschenbusch and placed increasing reliance upon social processes for salvation. When the personality is both individual and social, how was one to choose between the two? [31]

[28] *Ibid.*, pp. 318–26, 440.
[29] The growth of Greek dualism in Christian thought has been traced by Owens, *op. cit.*
[30] J. C. Pipes, "Motivation of Mountain Preachers," Transcript of *Conference on Motivation for the Ministry*, p. 11.
[31] See Andras Angyal's *Foundations for a Science of Personality* (New York: Commonwealth Fund, 1941).

One side of the dilemma may be seen in some inquirers at Graham's crusades who sought a church which was not preoccupied with literary sermons and "philosophizing." [32] The other side appears in the Appalachian church survey. Eighty-one per cent of Southern Baptist rural church members joined the church during a revival meeting. Out of 3,269 lines transcribed from weekly sermons by thirteen Southern Baptist ministers, only twenty-three were devoted to community morality. [33] One group cannot reconcile revival convictions with the social emphasis of their churches, while another finds revival in the church with no community consciousness.

Further study may reveal that many of the limitations of instant evangelism could be traced to this unnatural split between man's relation to God and man's relation to his neighbor.

Will the fourth period of national revival recover the solidarity of the great commandment (Mark 12:28–34)? Can this period of awakening produce the fruit of social enterprise that followed the first two revivals of our nation?

These are questions yet to be answered, but some developments already can be traced. One observable phenomenon is the rear-guard engagement between the spokesman for liberalism and conservatism. *Christianity Today* supports Graham and derides interdenominational social action. [34] *The Christian Century* upholds the social gospel and castigates "mass conversions." In an editorial marred by sarcasm and overstatement Graham was criticized for rejecting "by silence Niebuhr's plea to discuss the race question." [35] The editor ignored the revivalist's reference to race problems in his New York Crusade sermon on "The Offense of the Cross." [36]

[32] Ferm, *Persuaded to Live,* pp. 93, 169, 186.

[33] Earl D. C. Brewer, "Religion and the Churches," Research Memorandum, Southern Appalachian Studies, 1959–1961, p. 68.

[34] See for example, Editor Carl F. H. Henry's articles, "Has Anybody Seen 'Erape'?" *Christianity Today,* January 4 and 18, 1960. A more constructive approach may be found in his February 2, 1959 article, "Perspective for Social Action."

[35] *Christian Century,* May 29, 1959, p. 678. The editorial refers to Niebuhr's "Proposal to Billy Graham," *Christian Century,* August 8, 1956, pp. 921–22.

[36] Contained in Ferm, *Persuaded to Live,* p. 20.

Dr. Niebuhr's critique of Graham in *Life* magazine was moderate and honest. He evaluated Graham as a sincere exponent of the frontier evangelistic emphasis—that the old self must be shattered in a personal experience with Christ. Graham also honestly refers to "inquirers" rather than "converts." On social issues, Niebuhr states that "though [Graham] has sound personal views on racial segregation and other social issues of our time, he almost ignores all of them in his actual preaching." [37]

Another Union Seminary professor, Dr. John Bennett, had made favorable comments after Graham's 1954 visit: "He has made real progress on the race question. . . . He does not allow religion to be supported for the racial *status quo*." [38] Dr. Bennett made another statement which illustrated the danger of stereotyped thinking about revivalists: "Until his visit to Union I had classed him as a fundamentalist and socially reactionary evangelist." [39]

Unfortunately, some critics and some supporters of Graham are not as perceptive. *The Christian Century* preconceives Graham to be reactionary because he is a professional revivalist. Its position is echoed and magnified in liberal analyses such as Roy Eckardt's *The Surge of Piety in America*.[40]

On the opposing parapet, *Christianity Today* defends revivalism and the social *status quo*.[41] It is a position which is especially attractive to Southern conservatives.[42] For example, when a Negro leader of nonviolence, Martin Luther King, spoke at the Southern Baptist Seminary, the *Alabama Baptist* rebuked the Seminary for allowing discussion of "local situations." Speeches on controversial issues should be avoided, for "all things are not expedient." Furthermore, such "reckless moves . . . will be

[37] *Life*, July 1, 1957, p. 92.

[38] John Bennett, "Billy Graham at Union," *Union Seminary Quarterly Review* IX (May, 1954), 13.

[39] *Ibid.*, p. 12.

[40] Eckardt, *The Surge of Piety in America* (New York: Association Press, 1958), p. 111. In the same chapter Mr. Eckardt has some excellent observations, such as the need for a fellowship of believers.

[41] E.g., "Race Tensions and Social Change," *Christianity Today*, January 19, 1959.

[42] E.g., "Love of Freedom and Judicial Determination," *Christianity Today*, July 17, 1961, p. 22.

embarrassing to graduates in finding work." The editors wished that "brethren everywhere would get as excited over people being saved and knowing God's will for man's soul as they are for reformation here on this earth." [43] Thus the social consciousness of the young theological student is intimidated in the name of expediency and evangelism.

While the editors of liberal and conservative magazines maintain the old battle lines, Graham has advanced beyond their limited perspectives. He has combined the preaching of individual salvation with a policy of racial integration. Since 1954 he has refused to conduct a segregated revival campaign. This is an outstanding achievement. It has earned him the enmity of segregationists such as George Timmerman, lieutenant governor of South Carolina, when Graham was to address a rally on the Columbia Statehouse grounds in 1958. He was quoted as saying: "Billy Graham is well-known for his support of the program to mix the races in the South. As a Southerner, his endorsement of racial mixing has done more harm and his presence here on the Statehouse property will be misinterpreted as approval of that endorsement." [44]

Graham made the simple reply that his "only motive in going to South Carolina was to preach Christ and him crucified." But he did not preach it to a segregated audience. In 1960, Graham spoke to the Southern Baptist Convention in Miami Beach, Florida. His sermon included a challenge to change local racial attitudes and sectional patterns. Unless this were done quickly, Graham warned, our worldwide mission program among colored peoples would suffer irreparable damage.

To the Southerner, race relations are the most crucial of present social problems. The preaching and practice of Graham in this area is a living witness that revivalism and social problems can be related.

The witness of Graham is not an isolated one. He has had most vocal support from foreign missionaries. Among many denominations, these persons are thought of as the most dedi-

[43] *Alabama Baptist*, May 4, 1961, p. 3.
[44] *Courier-Journal*, October 12, 1958.

cated of evangelists. Their criticism of the racial *status quo* is especially effective, for some leaders have justified their social conservatism by a "zeal for souls." An honored and experienced missionary, Josephine Scaggs, rebuked the segregated policies of Southern Baptist institutions as she spoke on Foreign Missions' night of the 1961 Southern Baptist Convention. Miss Scaggs described invitations she had received to speak to Woman's Missionary Unions on the conversion of the heathen. In reply she offered to bring a native convert with her. The Southern women demurred. They honored the African in their hearts but not in their homes.

Whatever the social issue may be, the basic perspective must be personal salvation. Social drinking and segregation are denounced because they are stumbling blocks to Christian commitment and fellowship.

By centering upon salvation in Christ, evangelists may avoid two dangers as they seek to relate individual needs to social forces. The first danger is the idolatry of a single issue. Neither prohibition nor integration can be the major theme of evangelism. The recurring message of revival is Christ crucified. The second danger is silence on any social issue. Christ cannot be presented in isolation from life. To be revived, churches must be convicted of specific social sins.

There are barriers of suspicion and distrust that must be broken before revivals can again be accepted as personal and social forces for righteousness. Followers of nineteenth-century revivalism may doubt the evangelistic zeal of community-minded pastors. Sociologically-oriented pastors may look upon revivalists as hellfire antiquarians. Better understanding is needed. For example, a young pastor made an incidental reference to racial integration in his devotional talk to a denominational assembly. After the program, an executive in the field of evangelism approached him and the following conversation ensued:

EXECUTIVE: Young man, how many lost souls do you speak to every day?

PASTOR: Well, Sir, let me see. . . . I guess that I speak to at least three or four. I am part-time chaplain of the police court and probably see more derelict lives than any other pastor in the city.

EXECUTIVE (*surprised*): Oh, ah . . . is that so? Well, I try to speak to at least *one* lost soul a day myself.

PASTOR: That's fine, Sir (*pause*). Ah, I'm curious, how did you happen to ask me about my soul-winning?

EXECUTIVE: Oh, that. Well, you see, every time I hear one of you young fellows talk about all that liberal racial stuff, I want to know what you're *really* doing for the Lord. That's all.

PASTOR: I see. Thank you.

To combine prophetic religion with personal evangelism will involve the same kind of challenges that faced the revivalists of slaveholding days in America. These inner dilemmas of the church, described by Timothy Smith in *Revivalism and Social Reform*,[45] may be adapted to our day:

(1) Can a revivalist any more than a politician antagonize one section of the United States in pursuit of racial equality, prohibition of alcoholic beverages and gambling, or labor legislation?

(2) At what point does the solidarity of a denomination become less important than a clear witness against the sin of "sweat shops," segregation, or social drinking?

(3) Is the proper role of evangelized churches to be the regulation of individual conduct or the imposition of Christian principles upon social and legal institutions?

(4) Should the call for change and the exercise of discipline be an action of the local church, the association, a regional group, or a central denominational agency?

(5) Can Christians engage in peaceful demonstrations out of evangelistic zeal when it is feared that others will react to them with mob violence?

[45] *Op. cit.*, pp. 188 ff.

10
The Training of Evangelists

The first responsibility of pastors is not to evangelize but to produce an evangelizing congregation. Charles Spurgeon said that the one who converts a soul draws water from a fountain, but the one who trains evangelists digs a well from which thousands may drink. "Pastoral evangelism" is not the exclusive concern of those who hold the office of pastor. It is rather a quality of relationship toward lost people which is to be shared by all Christian leaders.

The Pastor's Example

The personal witness of a pastor provides inspiration and example for others. Unfortunately, some ministers do not embody in themselves the concern for others which they preach. How can they pass on that which they do not possess? For example, a preacher approached the chairman of deacons after a course of study on the "Ministry of Visitation." He began the conversation:

PASTOR: Brother A, here are the names of several persons whom the superintendent of the Sunday school and I have selected from the prospect file.
DEACON A: What do you want *me* to do with these cards?
PASTOR: As teacher of the men's Sunday school class, I thought you would be interested in these men. It will also be a fine chance for you to put into practice what we are learning in this study course.
DEACON A: I haven't time to visit.
PASTOR: Surely you can spare an hour or two a week. You know how important visitation is.
DEACON A: Yes, of course. Let's see those. Well, now, this man is

171

going to another church, and this one has been visited before. He
promises but never comes.

PASTOR: Select a few who seem to be better prospects to you.

DEACON A: Why don't you give these to all the Sunday school
classes? I've been visiting for years and no one has come yet. I've
been faithful when these people cared nothing for it. They ought to
visit me!

PASTOR: Brother A, I don't think you are in favor of our visitation
program.

The additional details of this argument might be supplied by
many pastors. What is wrong? The pastor urges, and Deacon A
resists. The former is all for a program. He will manipulate and
intimidate church leaders until they have to either give in or drop
out.

Later in the interview, the pastor asked Deacon A how long
it had been since he had visited for the cause of Christ and the
church. This further increased the man's defensiveness. Why
did not the pastor ask how long it had been since he had paid a
visit to the deacon? This faithful leader's plea for some pastoral
attention is ignored. It is not surprising that this minister can
find few visitors for the church. He demonstrates no personal
concern in his approach to lay leaders; how does he hope to
inspire them with love for people? If he tramples over the needs
of his own membership, how can he expect them to meet the
needs of those outside the church?

This same pastor may be very "evangelistic" in his own eyes.
He gives his body to be burned out in ceaseless visitation of the
unconverted. In time his interest wanes. Without love for people,
it cannot continue. Wearied and frustrated, he rebukes the congregation for their unconcern. Like a waterless cloud, he has
nothing to quench the thirst of his listeners and scolds them for
not giving a drink to others.

By contrast, a loving minister will refresh his people so that
they are revived and can minister to one another. There are many
channels of this grace. One of the deepest is pastoral visitation.
As a minister moves systematically among the homes of all his
people, they see in his actions the outreach of Christian care. Be-

cause they have received it from him, they can more readily express it themselves.

This spirit is also caught in the pastor's administrative relationships. As he seeks to introduce new talent into church committees, he shows that there are some new faces that can make a difference. At the same time he seeks to relieve responsibilities that are too burdensome upon faithful members. Compulsive persons will not like this, but most of the people will rejoice in a demonstration of his feeling that a program must serve people, including the needs of those who serve.

When lay leaders have seen and come to appreciate these pastoral attitudes of their minister, they are often willing to follow his leadership in visitation. This begins with instruction in personal interviewing. It is built upon the layman's respect for the way in which the minister has dealt with them. It has proved good in their own lives; now they might learn how to share it with others.

A Developing Interest

The people's response to a pastor's visitation may be developed through their organization for visitation before a revival, financial campaign, or family living institute. The pastor may spend several sessions in the training of deacons and church officers who would lead in this visitation. How may he present the personal aspects of evangelism to them?

Role-playing is one of the first teaching techniques that stimulates personal understanding. As a pastor, I set aside three evenings in which I would prepare the deacons through role-playing for visitation before a revival. During these sessions, I first acted as the person to be visited and invited a deacon to interview me before the entire group. We began:

DEACON: Hello, Mr. S, I wanted to visit you before our revival and
   invite you to attend.
PROSPECT: Oh, is that so? Why do you think I'd be interested in that?
DEACON: Well, now, *everybody* ought to be interested in religion.
   Don't you think so?
PROSPECT: I'm getting along pretty well as it is.

DEACON: I know, I know, but still, it's the kind of thing that everybody ought to do. . . .

The deacon was stuck. When I asked for comment, another deacon said: "He pitched it too much on what everybody ought to do." I replied: "That's right. How could he have made it more personal, more in keeping with the needs of this man?" Men began to suggest that the visitor should be one who knew the man and his interest or that the visitor explain his own interest in the church first. Perhaps the prospect would respond to another layman's reasons for relating to God.

After ten minutes of discussion, another deacon "visited" me:

DEACON: Mr. S, I'm glad to see you. Haven't seen you since we were at that party at Summit Heights!
PROSPECT: That's right. It was some party. What brings you by today?
DEACON: Well, I want to interest you in our church. You know we have a new preacher and he's doing a swell job. Takes lots of time to prepare his sermons too. You should come and hear him.
PROSPECT: Thanks. Maybe I will sometime.
DEACON: Good. I'll look forward to seeing you.

Several deacons thought that this was a good interview. I objected: "He made the preacher instead of the man's need for God the center of his appeal." The deacon defended himself: "Well, Preacher, we'll get them here and then you preach to them. That'll do it!" I was not so sure: "I doubt if he'll come. You met him with a big smile and bounced off too easily. I don't think you really caught him, do you?" The deacon, a most affable and expansive individual, grinned and confessed that maybe he was more interested in staying on the "right side" of the man than he was in confronting him with his need for the church.

On the second and third nights of training, deacons were paired with each other. One would be the visitor and the other would be the prospect. As the discussion progressed, the role-playing became an opportunity for some of the "prospects" to reveal some very specific problems about the church. This realism kept each man involved in the learning process. I acted as a mediator, clarifier, and summarizer.

When the training periods ended, the deacons chose partners, picked out prospect cards, and visited prospects on the following Sunday afternoon. At the next deacon's meeting each pair gave a report on this visitation. Most of the men reported a friendly reception from prospects, but some asked for help with "knotty" problems. Several men noted that prospects had promised to come but were not yet in church.

Their interviews had been too "easy." How could they reach a deeper level of motivation? Questions like these became the basis for a second type of training which can be offered in connection with the revival itself.

The Revival Instruction

A more comprehensive series of instruction in witnessing may be held a week before the meeting or during the morning or early evening hours of the revival week(s). All church members who would normally come to a service of revival are invited to attend these sessions on personal evangelism.

The instruction includes role-playing and the reading of verbatim interviews. I began such a morning meeting by reading interviews with a lay leader of the church. Some of the interviews in this book were used. After we had read the dialogue to the people, I asked the layman for his comments.

In response to a case of instant evangelism, he said: "Well, I didn't feel that you cared much about me" (I had read the part of the evangelist). I then asked members of the audience to suggest how they would have approached this individual. The responses on these and other occasions indicated that men and women are quite perceptive to personal needs. They seemed less occupied with correct doctrine or the quotation of Scripture verses than ministers are when this material is presented in a pastors' conference.

For the first session or two, few laymen responded unless called upon. But as the interviews aroused their interest, responses were more spontaneous. For example, after reading an interview with me, an officer of the women's organization asked: "But what about people like me who have always been in the church? How can we approach others who may feel outside the church—we don't understand them." I asked her to portray one outside the church while I acted like one who was a part of the congregation. After a few responses the woman found herself identifying with the "outsiders." She was so surprised by this that at one point she stopped to explain: "Now I don't *really* feel this way myself, but I've heard people say this."

The woman's response illustrates another aspect of the instruction—church people begin to understand themselves better. The questions and responses of these interviews stimulate them to ask how faith is real in their lives, how they justify their doctrines and the time they spend in the church. Out of this new self-understanding comes ability to enter into the doubts, sufferings, and insecurities of others. This is a precondition of pastoral evangelism.

Supervised Visitation

After the experience of reading interviews and participating in discussion, some members of the congregation begin to raise questions about their own visitation: "Well, Pastor, I visited Mr. O, and I wonder what you think of this. . . ." As the pastor listens to these illustrations, he may want to write them down later from memory or ask the laymen to do so. In this way he may know some of the specific problems of his people in witnessing. These cases can be the basis for future teachings on the "how-to" of evangelism.

The general interest in witnessing which comes through church officials and congregational meetings can be made specific in visitation which is supervised by the pastor. This may be done in two ways.

Personal guidance.—Personal guidance of individual laymen is the first step in pastoral supervision. Men often respond to a pastor's invitation to join him in visitation of a prospect for the church. On many occasions laymen will come to the minister for help in witnessing to some friend or acquaintance. Out of these individual concerns the pastor may develop a series of informal conferences in which the layman becomes the minister to one man and the pastor is his coach.

This method is especially helpful when a person has felt rejected by former ministers and is hostile to the church. The very office of the pastor creates a barrier. A layman has more ready access to the mind of such a man. One pastor saw this clearly. When he spoke to Mr. Booth, Mr. Booth always looked at the ground or pretended to be preoccupied. The main responsibility for winning Mr. Booth was, therefore, placed with one of his former high school friends, Mr. Conrad. Mr. Conrad was group captain in his Sunday school class. He had known Mr. Booth for ten years. He knew that Mr. Booth was the son of a prominent church family. When Mr. Booth had made an unwise marriage choice and was divorced, his family felt disgraced. Mr. Booth had retreated into periodic drinking which now threatened his stability on the job.

The pastor and Mr. Conrad decided that Mr. Booth should be approached through the Sunday school class. The first move was for Mr. Conrad to invite Mr. Booth to the weekly breakfast which members of the class held downtown on Monday morning. Although there was no organized program, the table talk included many references to the church and problems of religion in life. Mr. Booth came to the breakfast and was made welcome. No one asked him about the church, but Mr. Conrad noticed that he listened intently to all that was said about it.

Several days later, Mr. Booth asked his friend about an argued question at the breakfast. Mr. Conrad replied: "Well, I don't know too much about that point, but we have discussions like that all the time at our Sunday school class meeting. It's at my home next week. You be my guest."

At the class meeting, Mr. Booth sat in a corner and said little more than "How do you do." Mr. Conrad thought that he did appreciate the friendliness shown by the men as they greeted him. When one man asked Mr. Booth to come to their Sunday school class, Mr. Booth replied that he might.

Several weeks later, the Sunday school class undertook to rebuild the burned house of a widow. Mr. Conrad invited Mr. Booth to help. Since Mr. Booth was a skilled carpenter, he was well accepted by the other men and seemed to enjoy his contribution to the work. The one-room, frame house was completed in a week of after-hours' work by the men.

The Sunday school class met in a building several doors from the church. This was as close as Mr. Booth would come to the church for a long time. After six months of this, the class planned an Easter breakfast at the church. Mr. Booth attended this breakfast. It was his first time inside a church in years. The pastor spoke briefly at this breakfast. Mr. Booth looked at him during the talk. It was the first time he had looked up in this pastor's presence. He left before the pastor could shake hands with him.

By this time Mr. Booth had stopped drinking. He became engaged to a Christian girl in a nearby community. At the end of the year, the Sunday school teacher and Mr. Conrad had a problem for the pastor. Mr. Booth was now popular and regular in the class. Should he be put on a committee for a work project? It was decided that his name should be read out like any other class member. If he objected, Mr. Conrad would talk with him. If not, nothing would be said. Mr. Booth took the assignment and worked hard. He was so effective that men began to talk about him as a potential group captain.

About this time, Mr. Booth was married by the pastor of his fiancée in a neighboring community. She came to live in Mr. Booth's town and they began to attend morning church services. Through the ministry of Mr. Conrad and the interest and friendliness of others in the class, Mr. Booth was now able to face the pastor, the community, and the church for Christ. This was the time to meet him squarely with his need for an open dedication to God and the responsibilities of church membership.

Group conferences.—When it is time for a face-to-face encounter about conversion, Mr. Conrad will need more specific instruction. This may often be provided through group conferences which the pastor arranges for a selected group of lay evangelists. There should be six to twelve sessions of one and a half hours.[1] It would be best for these discussions to be held once a week, so that laymen would have time to think over the philosophy and practice the methodology of evangelism.

The first few sessions should be devoted to an explanation and discussion of the theology of evangelism. Good resource books include Culbert Rutenber's *The Reconciling Gospel;* T. A. Kantonen's *Theology of Evangelism;* and D. T. Niles' *That They May Have Life.* These are prepared for laymen; Rutenber's was specifically prepared for schools of evangelism.

The next section of the course would provide instruction in personal visitation. It would contain material in this or a similar volume on the process of salvation, varieties of conversion, and techniques of pastoral evangelism. Half the period might be devoted to lecture and half to discussion. Verbatim interviews would add clarity to both. These may be mimeographed and given to each pupil. It is best to follow the form given below from a layman's interview with a prospect. The layman received a "new family" card on April 25, and called by phone on April 28, to arrange for a visit. He walked into the man's yard on April 29, and found that he was mowing the grass.

VISITOR: Mr. Montgomery, I am visiting for Immanuel Church. We would like to enlist those who are new in our neighborhood. Would you tell me if you or your family attend church?
MR. M: No (*he didn't look happy*).
VISITOR: Do you have any interest in the church?
MR. M: No.
VISITOR: I see. Ah, let me get that rock out of your way. Is it all right to put it here in this rock garden?
MR. M: Well, I guess you could call it that—some day. . . .
VISITOR: You're just getting it started?
MR. M: Yes, but I don't have much time to work on it.

The interview continued for another page. The right-hand side of the paper is blank so that each person may write in his comments on the way he would have approached Mr. M and his re-

[1] A short-term course of instruction, "A Program of Person-to-Person Evangelism," has been prepared by the Division of Evangelism, Presbyterian Church, U. S., 341-B Ponce de Leon Avenue, N. E., Atlanta 8, Georgia.

action to Mr. M, response by response. When everyone has finished this exercise, the pastor leads a discussion of the interview by inviting each pupil in turn to read his comment on one response, if he wrote one. At the end of the hour and a half, the pastor would collect the papers. Six weeks later, he will give them the same interview again for their comments. A comparison of the two would probably indicate much growth.[2]

Again, role-playing is another way to be specific about people. For example, when a layman asks, "How would you answer a person who says . . . ?" the pastor may answer: "O.K. You be the person asking that question and I'll be the church visitor." After a few moment's mock conversation, the pastor can ask such questions as: "What do all of you see in this? What was I trying to do? How was this effective or ineffective? How did you feel, Mr. _____, as I talked this way to you?"

When others raise specific questions, the pastor may ask: "Would you help all of us this week by having an interview and writing down the actual words as nearly as you can? It may be a page, or it may be several pages. You need not include the person's name. We would like to discuss some of these at our meeting next week. Please bring them with you."

At the following meeting, some of the laymen will have interviews that are at least a page in length. This is enough for a beginning. Mr. X and Mr. Y should be asked to read Mr. Z's interview. This enables Mr. Z to hear himself from the mouth of another person. As Mr. X portrays Mr. Z, Mr. Y reads the responses of the person who is visited. As they read, the pastor, Mr. Z, or others may interrupt to make their comments.

By the end of the reading the group may be called on for general observations: How did the interview begin? How was Mr. Z received? What kind of relationship did he establish? How would you feel if you had been the prospect who was visited? In what ways would you approach this person differently? What about

---

[2] In a study that involved a similar procedure, Chester Raber found from 25 to 50 per cent improvement in the interviews of students in a fifteen-week seminary course. They had a better understanding of themselves and their pastoral role. They were more sympathetic with others and more competent in meeting specific personal needs.

the ending of the conversation? What follow-up might come from this?

Role-playing, the pupils' interviews, and their discussion will reveal some of the strengths and weaknesses of the group. Attention should be centered first upon attitudes and responses. Without personal insight attempts to perfect mechanical techniques will be futile.

Also, an interest in personal opinions will give laymen an opportunity to voice any doubts they may have about this plan of study. An occasion to express doubt and receive self-knowledge came when a middle-aged lady said: "I just don't see this 'pastoral' approach. Now when I visited a young mother last week I talked to her about her *soul*. Poor thing, she said she was all alone during the week with those two small children. I told her that it was a wonder she didn't cry all the time. She needed Jesus. That's what I talked to her about. She seemed so glad that I had come and wanted me to come back. Now, did I do right?"

Before the pastor could answer, a young woman said: "Why, Mrs. R, your visit, your presence was as important as what you said. You broke her loneliness, for you were someone with whom she could talk." A man said: "And how did you know she was lonely if you just talked about Jesus. You *did* have some personal interest in her, didn't you?"

"Oh, my, yes," replied Mrs. R, "but I mean that I didn't psychoanalyze her. I went there to present Christ." "Well, you did," answered the pastor, "although I doubt if you are aware of the way in which you presented him. Your tone of voice and your manner indicate a motherly interest in this young woman. You met her need for a *Christian* mother. Are you willing to be that to her?"

The smiles of others confirmed the pastor's opinion and encouraged Mrs. R to say "Well, ah, perhaps I was (*smiling*); at least I'm *old* enough to be her mother."

It is through this kind of group participation that the visitors learn to speak to one another in a spirit of love and self-control. Each visitor needs to know himself. The gospel itself is enough offense to the ungodly; it calls each man to recognize his unworthiness before God. The witness should not complicate or obscure this by injecting his personal difficulties. And, since most of us are blind to some of our most irritating mannerisms and assumptions, we need a truthful and trustworthy circle of friends to mirror these for us. To do this one must be committed deeply to evangelism, for who could require this analysis of another? It is only because these handpicked people share a common concern for a lost world that they speak face to face with such frankness and compassion.

A pastor may wonder whether he is capable of leading this level of personal interaction. He will be more secure and helpful if he has experienced a similar process in a seminary course, a pastors' conference, clinical training program, or a weekly discussion group led by a chaplain or a pastor trained in counseling.[3] Many recent seminary graduates will have participated in the write-up of verbatim interviews and group reviews of these. After someone has gently reminded a pastor that he is aggressive and manipulative, he may have more understanding and sympathy for his leaders when they reveal similar faults in their interviews. Most of all, if he has come through his own training period with acceptance and illumination, he will be more able to lead his own pastoral group through temporary periods of anxiety to new horizons of personal insight.

After the first interviews have been handed in by the laymen, several periods should be spent in group analysis of the interviews and the attitudes of the visitor and prospect. During the week between each period, the pastor should arrange to team up with one layman for an afternoon or evening of visitation. In the course of three or four weeks he could have visited with a dozen of his leaders. This number would probably be the largest that should be enrolled for a course which includes so much personal attention and individual participation.

As pastor and layman visit together, they may alternate in taking the lead. At the first home the pastor would take the initiative. When they return to the car they should take a few minutes

---

[3] Many types of training are advertised in the "Annual" (January) issue of *Pastoral Psychology*.

to let the layman evaluate the visit. What did he see in the home? What approach would he have used? What follow-up is indicated? At the next home, the layman would take the initiative, and so on.

By the time the pastor visits at least once with each layman, the group discussion could shift from visitor to prospect. This would be a person- and problem-centered approach. The layman should be asked to visit again—either alone or with another layman. Written interviews would be presented in the next few sessions with such questions as: What kind of person are you visiting? What is he trying to tell you? Did you observe the influence of other members of the family? Where should the church start in a ministry to these people? How will you explain their problems and possibilities to the teachers and officers who should assist in their care? What should Christ and the church mean to them? Where shall we start? What obstacles may we expect? In what ways are we likely to fail?

The Visitation Program

At the conclusion of the course of study, the laymen would again be asked to write their comments on a mimeographed verbatim interview. As the pastor compares these with earlier interviews, he can confirm or disprove his impressions gained from group discussions and individual visitation with each layman. He should summarize his views and tell the group that he would be glad to discuss these individually. Several weeks might pass by while the pastor continues the opportunity for private discussion with those who wish it. After such discussions he may present to the church nominating committee the names of those whom he wishes to be elected as visitors in evangelism.

These visitors would be used in at least two ways. First, there are opportunities for evangelistic visitation through a Sunday school class or other group organization of the church. A trained visitor would be an obvious selection for vice-president in charge of membership in either an Adult or a Young People's class. In this way evangelism might permeate the existing church structure.

Second, the pastor may call on the visitors for special or regular contacts with prospects. In one church, immediately upon the completion of a study program, the trained leaders began a visitation of all prospects. This was three weeks before a revival. Another church trained leaders in the early fall for monthly visitation throughout the year. The group met for dinner at 6:00 P.M., visited from 7:00 to 9:00 P.M., and returned to the church or to a home for a half-hour report meeting. Denominational literature describes various programs of this type.

All Christians are commanded to give witness of their faith, but not all are chosen to specifically represent the church in visitation. There are some exacting requirements of discipleship that precede selection as an evangelist.

Jesus described the nature of discipleship before he appointed the seventy to go before him into Samaria (Luke 9:51 to 10:24). In the same way, character and dedication are prerequisites today. Bigoted, quarrelsome, unscrupulous, hypocritical church members are no witnesses *for* Christ. They need redemption and more instruction in the meaning of Christian discipleship. Neurotic, compulsive visitors will distort the image of Christianity. Sometimes members will warn: "Preacher, Mrs. L is a good woman, but she is so nervous and high-strung. I don't think she'd do anyone good by a visit."

How is the pastor to know who is qualified? His visitation and personal interest in the membership will help to answer this. For example, a pastor was stopped after a revival instruction period by Miss O, a nineteen-year-old, who asked how she might enlist more leaders in her youth council. The pastor invited her to the church office where she might discuss all her concerns. After talking about organizational problems, she said, "Another thing—I want to know how to talk about Christ. When I try, it seems that they shy away from me (*pause*).

PASTOR: Go on.
MISS O: Well, I would just like to tell them how wonderful Jesus is.
PASTOR: How have you seen this in your own life?
MISS O: Ah, I guess most of all in giving me some Christian young

people to be with. I never had much of this before, you know.

PASTOR: Yes. And now you'd like to share this with others?

MISS O: Uh-huh. I see that some kids I work with are lonesome like I used to be, but I get so embarrassed talking about religion. You know—I mean, well, I was never brought up to talk about very personal things, and never about God or the church.

As the conversation continued, the pastor saw in Miss O a sensitivity to the deeper needs of her associates and an awareness of the ways by which Christian faith and fellowship had met the same needs in her own life. She would be a good prospect for training in evangelism.

These personal contacts also alert the pastor to unsuitable choices for training. One layman appeared in church to be a distinguished, prosperous gentleman. But when the pastor visited in his home, he had the uneasy feeling that a play was being presented to impress him. Husband and wife seemed *so* nice. But they would not discuss their own commitment to the church or the significance of Christ in their own lives. As the pastor became better acquainted in the community, he found that the husband had a reputation for unscrupulous and unfeeling business practices. The wife appeared in both community and church as a social climber. This couple was already an embarrassment to thoughtful Christians.

In addition to these individual contacts, the pastor can also note the responses of members to the open instruction on evangelism during an organizational meeting or a revival. Those who show understanding and interest should be encouraged to work more closely with the pastor in an intensive course of study.

The Continuing Commission

The requirements of personal evangelism are exacting. The man who is called to the office of pastor cannot fulfil it alone. He needs many laymen who also can be personal ambassadors of Christ Jesus. The appeal of God is made through every person whose righteous life and perceptive speech awakens the concern of another for salvation. Pastoral evangelism is a continuing commission for every concerned person in the congregation of Christ.

Appendix

Topics for Discussion
in an Inquirer's Class

1. What Is the Gospel and How Do We Interpret It?

NILES, DANIEL T., *Reading the Bible Today*. New York: Association Press, 1955.

HUNTER, ARCHIBALD M., *The Message of the New Testament*. Philadelphia: The Westminster Press, 1944.

HORDERN, WILLIAM. *A Layman's Guide to Protestant Theology*. New York: The Macmillan Co., 1955.

KNUDSON, ALBERT C. *Basic Issues in Christian Thought*. New York: Abingdon Press, 1950.

BRUNNER, H. EMIL. *Our Faith*. New York: Charles Scribner's Sons, 1949.

RUTENBER, CULBERT G. *The Price and the Prize*. Philadelphia: Judson Press, 1953.

————. *The Reconciling Gospel*. Philadelphia: Judson Press, 1960.

GREEN, JOSEPH F., JR. *Faith to Grow On*. Nashville: Broadman Press, 1960.

2. How We Got Our Bible and How It Can Be Understood

NILES, DANIEL T. *Reading the Bible Today*. New York: Association Press, 1955.

MILLER, PARK HAYS. *How to Study and Use the Bible*. Massachusetts: W. A. Wilde Co., 1949.

HERKLOTS, H. G. G. *How Our Bible Came to Us*. New York: Oxford University Press, 1954.

Our Bible—How It Came to Us (film). New York: American Bible Society.

ROWLEY, H. H. *Relevance of the Bible*. Illinois: Alec R. Allensen, Inc., 1948.

BRUCE, F. F. *The English Bible: A History of Translations*. New York: Oxford University Press, 1961.

BROWN, ROBERT M. *The Bible Speaks to You*. Philadelphia: The Westminster Press, 1955.

DANA, H. E. and GLAZE, R. E., JR. *Interpreting the New Testament*. Nashville: Broadman Press, 1961.

3. What Is the Church and How Did Our Denomination Develop?

GUSTAFSON, JAMES M. *Treasure in Earthen Vessels: The Church as a Human Community*. New York: Harper & Brothers, 1961.

BRIGHT, JOHN. *The Kingdom of God*. New York: Abingdon Press, 1953.

MINEAR, PAUL. *Jesus and His People*. New York: Association Press, 1956.

BROWN, ROBERT M. *The Significance of the Church*. Philadelphia: The Westminster Press, 1956.

BAINTON, ROLAND H. *The Church of Our Fathers*. New York: Charles Scribner's Sons, 1941.

LATOURETTE, K. S. *The Christian World Mission in Our Day*. New York: Harper & Brothers, 1954.

BRUCE, F. F. *The Spreading Flame*. Grand Rapids: William B. Eerdmans Publishing Co., 1953.

McCALL, DUKE K. (ed.). *What Is the Church?* Nashville: Broadman Press, 1958.

4. The Meaning and Manner of Prayer and Worship

DAY, ALBERT E. *An Autobiography of Prayer*. New York: Harper & Brothers, 1952.

DICKS, RUSSELL L. *Comfort Ye My People*. New York: The Macmillan Co., 1947.

FOSDICK, HARRY EMERSON. *The Meaning of Prayer*. New York: Association Press, 1915.

FERRE, NELS F. S. *Strengthening the Spiritual Life*. New York: Harper & Brothers, 1951.

HEILER, FRIEDRICH. *Prayer: A Study in the History and Psychology of Religion*. New York: Oxford University Press, 1932.

CASTEEL, JOHN L. *Rediscovering Prayer*. New York: Association Press, 1955.

BUTTRICK, GEORGE A. *Prayer*. New York: Abingdon Press, 1942.

CASTEEL, JOHN L. (ed.). *Spiritual Renewal Through Personal Groups*. New York: Association Press, 1957.

5. The Common Ventures of Life: Birth, Baptism, Vocation, Marriage, Sickness, Bereavement, Retirement, Death

TRUEBLOOD, ELTON. *The Common Ventures of Life*. New York: Harper & Brothers, 1949.

────── and TRUEBLOOD, PAULINE. *The Recovery of Family Life*. New York: Harper & Brothers, 1953.

YOUNG, RICHARD K. and MEIBURG, ALBERT L. *Spiritual Therapy: How the Physician, Psychiatrist and Minister Collaborate in Healing*. New York: Harper & Brothers, 1960.

CLARK, RANDOLPH LEE, JR. and CUMLEY, RUSSELL W. (eds.). *The Book of Health*. Princeton: D. Van Nostrand Co., Inc., 1953.

ROGERS, WILLIAM F. *Ye Shall Be Comforted*. Philadelphia: The Westminster Press, 1950.

WYNN, J. CHARLES. *How Christian Parents Face Family Problems*. Philadelphia: The Westminster Press, 1955.

TRENT, ROBBIE. *Your Child and God*. New York: Harper & Brothers, 1952.

BAILEY, D. S. *The Mystery of Love and Marriage*. New York: Harper & Brothers, 1952.

OATES, WAYNE and SOUTHARD, SAMUEL. "Marriage Counseling Kit" (filmstrips). Hollywood: Family Films, Inc.

HOWE, REUEL L. *The Creative Years*. Greenwich: Seabury Press, 1958.

FOSDICK, H. E. *On Being a Real Person*. New York: Harper & Brothers, 1943.

DUVALL, EVELYN M. and HILL, REUBEN. *When You Marry* (rev. ed.). New York: Association Press, 1953.

MAVES, PAUL B. *The Best Is Yet to Be*. New York: The Westminster Press, 1951.

SHERRILL, LEWIS J. *The Struggle of the Soul*. New York: The Macmillan Co., 1952.

MILLER, ALEXANDER. *Christian Faith and My Job*. New York: Association Press, 1946.

CALHOUN, ROBERT L. *God and the Day's Work*. New York: Association Press, 1957.

6. The Christian as a Minister of Reconciliation in His Community and in the World

RAUSCHENBUSCH, WALTER. *A Rauschenbusch Reader*. New York: Harper & Brothers, 1957.

MASTON, T. B. *The Bible and Race.* Nashville: Broadman Press, 1959.

MURRAY, JOHN. *The Daily Life of the Christian.* New York: Philosophical Library, Inc., 1955.

KEE, HOWARD C. *Making Ethical Decisions.* Philadelphia: The Westminster Press, 1957.

MCCARTHY, RAYMOND G. and DOUGLAS, EDGAR M. *Alcohol and Social Responsibility: a New Educational Approach.* New York: Thomas Y. Crowell Co., 1949.

STOLL, GEORGE. *Laymen at Work,* ed. ALBERT L. MEIBERG. New York: Abingdon Press, 1956.

ASHMORE, HARRY. *An Epitaph for Dixie.* New York: W. W. Norton & Co., Inc., 1958.

BLACKWELL, GORDON, *et al. Church and Community in the South.* Richmond: John Knox Press, 1949.

WOODWARD, C. VAN. *The Strange Career of Jim Crow,* rev. ed. New York: Oxford University Press, 1958.

WHALE, J. S. *The Christian Answer to the Problem of Evil.* New York: Abingdon Press, 1936.

LONG, EDWARD LEROY, JR. *Conscience and Compromise.* Philadelphia: The Westminster Press, 1954.

KNOX, JOHN (ed.). *Religion and the Present Crisis.* Chicago: University of Chicago Press, 1942.

Another list of books for small group discussions may be found in John Casteel's *Spiritual Renewal Through Personal Groups.* pp. 215 ff.

Bibliography

ABELL, AARON I. *The Urban Impact on American Protestantism*. Cambridge: Harvard University Press, 1943.

ACKERMAN, NATHAN W. *Psychodynamics of Family Life*. New York: Basic Books, Inc., 1958.

ALLPORT, GORDON. *The Individual and His Religion*. New York: The Macmillan Co., 1950.

ANDREASEN, JACOB. *Lutherans and Conversion*. Minneapolis: T. S. Denison & Co., 1955.

ANGYAL, ANDRAES. *Foundations for a Science of Personality*. New York: Commonwealth Fund, 1941.

ARCHIBALD, ARTHUR C. *Establishing the Converts*. Philadelphia: Judson Press, 1952.

————. *Man to Man*. Nashville: Broadman Press, 1956.

————. *New Testament Evangelism: How It Works Today*. Philadelphia: Judson Press, 1946.

ARNDT, WILLIAM F. and GINGRICH, F. WILBUR. *A Greek-English Lexicon of the New Testament and Other Early Christian Literature*. Translation and adaptation of Walter Bauer. Chicago: University of Chicago Press, 1957.

BAILEY, D. S. *Sexual Relations in Christian Thought*. New York: Harper & Brothers, 1959.

BAILLIE, D. M. *God Was in Christ*. New York: Charles Scribner's Sons, 1948.

Baptist Confession of Faith and a Manual of Church Discipline. Charleston, S. C.: W. Riley, 1831.

BARCLAY, WILLIAM. *A New Testament Wordbook*. New York: Harper & Brothers, 1955.

BARTH, KARL. *Church Dogmatics*. New York: Charles Scribner's Sons, 1955.

————. *The Teaching of the Church Regarding Baptism*. London: SCM Press, 1954.

BEARD, CHARLES A. *The Rise of American Civilization*. New York: The Macmillan Co., 1927.

BEGBIE, HAROLD. *Souls in Action*. New York: Hodder & Stoughton, 1911.

————. *Twice-born Men: a Clinic in Regeneration*. Westwood, N. J.: Fleming H. Revell Co., 1909.

190

BOISEN, ANTON. *The Exploration of the Inner World*. New York: Willett, Clark & Co., 1936.

BONHOEFFER, DIETRICH. *The Cost of Discipleship*. New York: The Macmillan Co., 1949.

BOWERS, PALMER. "An Evaluation of the Billy Graham Greater Louisville Evangelistic Crusade." Unpublished Master's thesis, Southern Baptist Theological Seminary, Louisville, Kentucky, 1959.

BOYLE, JOHN. "Group Dynamics in the Care of New Members." Unpublished Master's thesis, Southern Baptist Theological Seminary, Louisville, Kentucky, 1955.

BRUNNER, EMIL. *Justice and the Social Order*. New York: Harper & Brothers, 1945.

———. *The Christian Doctrine of Creation and Redemption*. Philadelphia: The Westminster Press, 1952.

———. *The Divine Imperative*. Philadelphia: The Westminster Press, 1947.

———. *The Mediator*. Philadelphia: The Westminster Press, 1947.

BULTMANN, RUDOLF. *The Theology of the New Testament*. New York: Charles Scribner's Sons, 1951.

BUNYAN, JOHN. *The Pilgrim's Progress*. New York: Century Company, 1900.

BUSHNELL, HORACE. *Christian Nurture*. New Haven: Yale University Press, 1948.

BUTTRICK, GEORGE A. (ed.). *The Interpreter's Bible*. 12 vols. New York: Abingdon Press, 1951.

CALVIN, JOHN. *Commentary on the Epistles of Paul the Apostle to the Corinthians*. Grand Rapids: Wm. B. Eerdmans Publishing Co., 1948.

CARNELL, E. J. *Christian Commitment*. New York: The Macmillan Co., 1957.

CARTWRIGHT, PETER. *Autobiography*. Nashville: Abingdon Press, 1956.

CLARK, E. T. *The Psychology of Religious Awakening*. New York: The Macmillan Co., 1929.

CLARK, WALTER HOUSTON. *The Psychology of Religion*. New York: The Macmillan Co., 1958.

COE, GEORGE A. *Education in Religion and Morals*. Westwood, N. J.: Fleming H. Revell Co., 1904.

COLE, STEWART G. *The History of Fundamentalism*. New York: Richard R. Smith, Inc., 1931.

CONNER, W. T. *The Gospel of Redemption*. Nashville: Broadman Press, 1945.

COX, NORMAN WADE. *Encyclopedia of Southern Baptists*. Nashville: Broadman Press, 1958.

CROSS, WHITNEY R. *The Burned-over District*. Ithaca: Cornell University Press, 1950.

CROUCH, AUSTIN. *The Plan of Salvation*. Nashville: Sunday School Board of the Southern Baptist Convention, 1924.

DILLISTONE, F. W. *The Significance of the Cross*. Philadelphia: The Westminster Press, 1944.

DOBBINS, GAINES S. *Winning the Children.* Nashville: Broadman Press, 1953.

————. *The Churchbook.* Nashville: Broadman Press, 1951.

DODDRIDGE, PHILIP. *Rise and Progress of Religion in the Soul.* New York: D. Appleton & Co., 1835.

DONIGER, SIMON (ed.). *Evangelism and Pastoral Psychology.* Great Neck, New York: Pastoral Psychology Press, 1956.

ECKARDT, A. ROY. *The Surge of Piety in America.* New York: Association Press, 1958.

EDGE, FINDLEY B. *Teaching for Results.* Nashville: Broadman Press, 1956.

EDWARDS, JONATHAN. *The Narrative,* JAMES STEWART (ed.). Grand Rapids: Kregel Publications, 1957.

FAIRCHILD, ROY and WYNN, JOHN. *Families in the Church: a Protestant Survey.* New York: Association Press, 1961.

FERM, ROBERT O. *Persuaded to Live.* Westwood, N. J.: Fleming H. Revell Co., 1958.

————. *The Psychology of Christian Conversion.* Westwood, N. J.: Fleming H. Revell Co., 1959.

FICHTER, JOSEPH H. *Social Relations in the Urban Parish.* Chicago: University of Chicago Press, 1954.

FINNEY, CHARLES G. *Lectures on Revivals of Religion.* Cambridge: Harvard University Press, 1960.

FOSTER, GEORGE. *The Finality of the Christian Religion.* Chicago: University of Chicago Press, 1906.

GARRISON, W. E. *The March of Faith.* New York: Harper & Brothers, 1933.

GAUSTAD, E. S. *The Great Awakening in New England.* New York: Harper & Brothers, 1957.

GERSTNER, JOHN H. *Steps to Salvation: the Evangelistic Message of Jonathan Edwards.* Philadelphia: The Westminster Press, 1959.

GILMORE, A. (ed.). *Christian Baptism.* Philadelphia: Judson Press, 1959.

GREEN, JOSEPH F., JR. *Faith to Grow On.* Nashville: Broadman Press, 1960.

HARRISON, E. MYERS and WILSON, W. L. *How to Win Souls.* Wheaton: Van Kampen, 1952.

HAVIGHURST, ROBERT J. *Human Development and Education.* New York: Longmans, Green & Co., 1953.

HENRY, C. F. H. *Evangelical Responsibility in Contemporary Theology.* Grand Rapids: Wm. B. Eerdmans Publishing Co., 1953.

————. *Christian Personal Ethics.* Grand Rapids: Wm. B. Eerdmans Publishing Co., 1957.

HEPPE, HEINRICH. *Reformed Dogmatics.* London: George Allen & Unwin, 1950.

HERBERG, WILL. *Protestant-Catholic-Jew.* New York: Doubleday & Co., 1955.

HILLYER, S. G. *Reminiscences of Georgia Baptists.* Atlanta. Foote & Davies, 1902.

HISCOX, EDWARD T. *The Standard Manual for Baptist Churches*. Philadelphia: Judson Press, 1903.

HODGE, CHARLES. *Systematic Theology*. New York: Charles Scribner's Sons, 1898.

HOLLIDAY, JOHN FRANCIS. *Life from Above*. Toronto: Evangelical Publishers, 1957.

HOLLINGSHEAD, AUGUST. *Elmtown's Youth*. New York: John Wiley & Sons, Inc., 1949.

HOMRIGHAUSEN, ELMER G. *Choose Ye This Day*. Philadelphia: The Westminster Press, 1943.

HOPKINS, C. H. *The Rise of the Social Gospel in American Protestantism, 1865–1915*. New Haven: Yale University Press, 1940.

HOWE, REUEL L. *Man's Need and God's Action*. Greenwich, Connecticut: The Seabury Press, 1953.

HUNTER, A. M. *Interpreting Paul's Gospel*. Philadelphia: The Westminster Press, 1955.

JAMES, WILLIAM. *The Varieties of Religious Experience*. New York: Modern Library, 1902.

JOHNSON, AUBREY. *Vitality of the Individual in the Thought of Ancient Israel*. Cardiff: University of Wales Press, 1949.

JOHNSON, L. D. "Psychological Study of Christian Conversion." Unpublished Th.D. dissertation, Southern Baptist Seminary, Louisville, Kentucky, 1942.

KANTONEN, T. A. *The Theology of Evangelism*. Philadelphia: Muhlenberg Press, 1954.

KITTEL, GERHARD. *Bible Key Words*. 3 vols. Translated and edited by J. R. COATES. New York: Harper & Brothers, 1952–61.

KNIGHT, ALLAN R. and SCHROEDEN, GORDON H. *Your New Life*. Philadelphia: American Baptist Publication Society, 1947.

LATOURETTE, K. S. "Distinctive Features," *Evangelism*. ("Madras Series.") Vol. III. New York: International Missionary Council, 1939.

———. *The Nineteenth Century Outside Europe*. New York: Harper & Brothers, 1961.

LAWRENCE, WILLIAM. *Fifty Years*. New York: Houghton Mifflin Co., 1923.

LENSKI, GERHARD. *The Religious Factor*. New York: Doubleday & Co., 1961.

LIGON, ERNEST. *Parent Roles: His and Hers*. Schenectady, New York: Ernest Ligon, 1959.

McGIFFERT, ARTHUR C. *The Rise of Modern Religious Ideas*. New York: The Macmillan Co., 1915.

MacIVER, ROBERT M. *Society*. New York: The Macmillan Co., 1938.

MACKINTOSH, H. R. *The Christian Experience of Forgiveness*. London: James Nisbet & Co., 1927.

McLOUGHLIN, WILLIAM G., JR. *Billy Graham: Revivalist in a Secular Age*. New York: The Ronald Press, 1960.

———. *Modern Revivalism*. New York: The Ronald Press, 1958.

MANSON, T. W. *Ministry and Priesthood: Christ's and Ours*. Richmond: John Knox, 1958.

MARTY, MARTIN. *The New Shape of American Religion.* New York: Harper & Brothers, 1959.

MASLOW, ABRAHAM H. (ed.). *New Knowledge in Human Values.* New York: Harper & Brothers, 1959.

MATHEWS, SHAILER. *The Church and the Changing Order.* New York: The Macmillan Co., 1907.

MATTHEWS, C. E. *A Church Revival.* Nashville: Broadman Press, 1955.

MAY, HENRY F. *Protestant Churches and Industrial America.* New York: Harper & Brothers, 1949.

MOLLEGEN, ALBERT T. *Christianity and Modern Man.* Indianapolis: Bobbs-Merrill Co., 1961.

MOODY, DWIGHT L. *Glad Tidings.* New York: E. B. Treat & Co., 1876.

————. *Great Joy.* New York: E. B. Treat & Co., 1877.

MULLINS, EDGAR YOUNG. *The Christian Religion in Its Doctrinal Expression.* Philadelphia: Judson Press, 1917.

————. *Talks on Soul Winning.* Nashville: Convention Press, 1920.

NASH, ARNOLD (ed.). *Protestant Thought in the Twentieth Century: Whence and Whether?* New York: The Macmillan Co., 1951.

NEVIN, J. W. *The Anxious Bench.* Chambersburg, Pennsylvania: Publication Office, German Reformed Church, 1844.

NIEBUHR, REINHOLD. *The Nature and Destiny of Man.* New York: Charles Scribner's Sons, 1941.

————. *The Self and the Dramas of History.* New York: Charles Scribner's Sons, 1955.

NILES, D. T. *That They May Have Life.* New York: Harper & Brothers, 1951.

OATES, WAYNE E. *Christ and Selfhood.* New York: Association Press, 1961.

OGBURN, W. F. *Social Change with Respect to Culture and Original Nature.* New York: Huebsch, B. W., 1922.

OLIVE, HOWARD. "The Development of the Evangelistic Invitation." Unpublished Master's thesis, Southern Baptist Theological Seminary, Louisville, Kentucky, 1958.

OMAN, JOHN. *Grace and Personality.* New York: Association Press, 1961.

OWENS, D. R. G. *Body and Soul.* Philadelphia: The Westminster Press, 1956.

PARSONS, TALCOTT. *The Structure of Social Action.* New York: Free Press of Glencoe, 1948.

PATERSON, W. P. *Conversion.* London: Hodder & Stoughton, 1939.

PIAGET, JEAN. *The Moral Judgment of the Child.* New York: Free Press of Glencoe, 1948.

POWELL, SIDNEY W. *Where Are the Converts?* Nashville: Broadman Press, 1958.

RAUSCHENBUSCH, WALTER. *Christianity and the Social Crisis.* New York: The Macmillan Co., 1907.

————. *A Gospel for the Social Awakening.* Compiled by B. E. Mays. New York: Association Press, 1950.

ROBERTSON, A. T. *Word Pictures in the New Testament*. Nashville: Sunday School Board of the Southern Baptist Convention, 1930.

ROBINSON, JOHN A. T. *The Body: a Study in Pauline Theology*. Chicago: H. Regnery, 1952.

ROWLEY, H. H. *The Unity of the Bible*. Philadelphia: The Westminster Press, 1955.

SALZMAN, JEAN. "The Psychology of Religion and Ideological Conversion." *Psychiatry*, XVI.

SCHNEIDER, LOUIS and DORNBUSCH, SANFORD. *Popular Religion: American Inspirational Literature*. Chicago: University of Chicago Press, 1958.

SHERRILL, LEWIS J. *The Opening Doors of Childhood*. New York: The Macmillan Co., 1939.

SIMS, N. L. R. *The Problem of Social Change*. New York: Thomas Y. Crowell Co., 1939.

SIMS, WALTER HINES. *Baptist Hymnal*. Nashville: Convention Press, 1956.

SMITH, G. B. *Social Idealism and the Changing Theology: a Study of the Ethical Aspects of Christian Doctrine*. New York: The Macmillan Co., 1913.

SMITH, H. SHELTON; HANDY, ROBERT T.; and LOETSCHER, L. A. *American Christianity*. New York: Charles Scribner's Sons, 1960.

SMITH, HILRIE S. *Changing Conceptions of Original Sin*. New York: Charles Scribner's Sons, 1955.

SMITH, TIMOTHY L. *Revivalism and Social Reform*. New York: Abingdon Press, 1957.

SOUTHARD, SAMUEL (ed.). "Transcript of Conference on Motivation for the Ministry." Louisville: Southern Baptist Seminary, 1959.

SPENCER, ICHABOD. *Pastor's Sketches;* or *Conversations with Anxious Enquirers Respecting the Way of Salvation*. New York: M. W. Rodd, 1853.

SPURGEON, C. H. *The Soul-Winner*. Westwood, N. J.: Fleming H. Revell Co., 1895.

————. *Twelve Sermons on the Plan of Salvation*. Westwood, N. J.: Fleming H. Revell Co., n. d.

STARBUCK, EDWIN D. *The Psychology of Religion*. New York: Charles Scribner's Sons, 1901.

STEIN, MAURICE R., *et al. Identity and Anxiety*. New York: Free Press of Glencoe, Inc., 1960.

STEWART, JAMES S. *A Man in Christ*. New York: Harper & Brothers, 1935.

STRONG, A. H. *Systematic Theology*. New York: Press of E. R. Andrews, 1886.

SWEET, W. W. *The Baptists*. New York: Henry Holt & Co., 1931.

———— (ed.). *The Presbyterians: Religion on the American Frontier, 1783–1840*. New York: Harper & Brothers, 1936.

TAYLOR, VINCENT. *Atonement in the New Testament Teaching*. Naperville, Illinois: Alec R. Allenson, Inc., 1954.

————. *Forgiveness and Reconciliation*. London: The Macmillan Co., 1941.

THAYER, J. H. *A Greek-English Lexicon of the New Testament*. New York: The American Book Co., 1886.

THELEN, MARY. *Man as Sinner in Contemporary American Realistic Theology*. New York: King's Crown Press, 1946.

THORNTON, L. S. *The Common Life in the Body of Christ*. Naperville, Illinois: Alec R. Allenson, Inc., 1950.

TORREY, R. A. *How to Work for Christ*. Westwood, N. J.: Fleming H. Revell Co., 1901.

TRINTERUD, L. J. *The Forming of an American Tradition*. Philadelphia: The Westminster Press, 1949.

TRUEBLOOD, DAVID ELTON. *The Yoke of Christ*. New York: Harper & Brothers, 1958.

TUCKER, W. J. *My Generation: an Autobiographical Interpretation*. New York: Houghton Mifflin Co., 1919.

TYLER, ALICE F. *Freedom's Ferment: Phases of American Social History to 1860*. Minneapolis: University of Minnesota, 1944.

WALKER, JAMES. *Philosophy of the Plan of Salvation*. Boston: Gould and Tincton, 1874.

WARFIELD, BENJAMIN. *The Plan of Salvation*. Grand Rapids: Wm. B. Eerdmans Publishing Co., 1942.

WARNER, W. LLOYD. *Social Class in America*. New York: Harper & Brothers, 1960.

WEISBERGER, B. A. *They Gathered at the River*. Boston: Little, Brown & Co., 1958.

WEISENBURGER, FRANCIS. *Ordeal of Faith*. New York: Philosophical Library, 1959.

WESLEY, JOHN. *The Journal of the Rev. John Wesley*. London: The Epworth Press, 1938.

————. *The Works of the Rev. John Wesley*. New York: Eaton & Mains, 1850.

WEST, JAMES. *Plainville, U. S. A.* New York: Columbia University Press, 1945.

WHITE, R. E. O. *The Biblical Doctrine of Initiation*. Grand Rapids: Wm. B. Eerdmans Publishing Co., 1960.

WINSLOW, OLA E. *Jonathan Edwards, 1703–1758*. New York: The Macmillan Co., 1940.

WINTER, GIBSON. *The Surburban Captivity of the Churches*. Garden City: Doubleday & Co., 1961.

WOOD, A. S. *The Inextinguishable Blaze*. Grand Rapids: Wm. B. Eerdmans Publishing Co., 1960.

World Council of Churches. "Theological Reflection on the Work of Evangelism." W.C.C. Bulletin Vol. V. No. 1–2. November, 1959.

YODER, GIDEON G. *The Nurture and Evangelism of Children*. Scottdale, Pennsylvania: Herald Press, 1959.

Index